Ann Belford Ulanov

The Psychoid, Soul and Psyche: Piercing Space-Time Barriers

Ann Belford Ulanov

The Psychoid, Soul and Psyche: Piercing Space-Time Barriers

DAIMON
Verlag

ACKNOWLEDGMENTS

Daimon Verlag and the author would like to thank the following
for their generous support in making this book possible:
Thomas F. Beech, Ray Chambers, Bob Boisture
and the Stable Foundation.

Cover art by Barry Ulanov
Photograph of the author © Catherine Frantzis

ISBN 978-3-85630-768-4

With deep gratitude to the three analysts
with whom I have worked in my personal analysis.

Contents

1. The Psychoid, Psyche and Soul:
Piercing Space-Time Barriers

A sentence in Jung's paper "Soul and Death" struck into me because it connected with a clinical experience that was profound. Jung was addressing the difference between consciousness whose "limitation ... in space and time is such an overwhelming reality" that when it is "annulled," as it was in that clinical experience, it is of "the highest theoretical significance" and the "annulling factor would be the psyche, since space-time would attach to it at most as a relative and conditioned quality." But, Jung goes further, "Under certain conditions it [psyche] could even break through the barriers of space and time precisely because of a quality essential to it ... its relatively trans-spatial and trans-temporal nature." Jung urges, "The possible transcendence of space-time ... is of such incalculable import that it should spur the spirit of research to the greatest effort" (Jung 1934/1960, para 813; also cited in Bright 20014, 87).

This book is an effort to contribute to such research. Jung was discussing the space-time barriers in relation to telepathy. I am discussing them in relation to clinical experience of the psychoid quality of unconscious processes. Further, penetrating space-time barriers links to Jung's looking for his lost soul, as recounted in *The Red Book* (Jung 2009, 232). Without soul, he lost not only his capacity to annul the space-time barrier, but also lost the aliveness of his everyday life.

Both Jung and Freud thought our projections of psyche and soul into religious categories, let alone political, philosophical or cultural institutions, that is, into containers 'outside' the psyche, had fallen away. Where had all that projected energy gone? It fell into our human psyche and the new discipline of psychoanalysis was the result. For Freud this meant getting rid of religion, for Jung, this meant investigating what he eventually called the ultra-violet spiritual pole of the archetype and the God-image and God beyond it.

In his *Liber Novus*, a pivotal transition happens to Jung, changing his initial project of reanimating religious traditions by discerning the correspondence of the truth of their symbols to images arising in our psyche. He now sees the human psyche is itself the site of transformation: "the spirit of the depths burst forth and led me to the site of the innermost" (Jung 2009, 239; see also 252 n.211, 253, and n227, 228; see also Jung 1953, para 7). Psyche/soul is now a space where transforming of us happens (or fails to) and that relates to what animates the whole world, for "*the psychology of the individual, corresponds to the psychology of the nation. What the nation does is done also by each individual, and so long as the individual does it, the nation also does it.* Only the change in the attitude of the individual is the beginning of the change in the psychology of the nation" (Jung 2009, 253 n221 and in Jung 1953/1966, para 7, his italics; see also Jaffé 1963, 132).

Psyche and Soul

Psyche is all the processes conscious and unconscious which enable or disable us to be a person connected to self, to others and to what transcends psyche. Psyche mediates reality, adding a psychical line of interpretation to traditional hermeneutics (Ulanov and Ulanov, 1975, 81-82). Soul is that willingness to be such a person related to self and others and to the beyond, the something more in us that longs for, desires both something beyond and dwelling in the quotidian. Jung writes, "it [the soul] has the dignity of an entity endowed with, and conscious of, a relationship to deity" (Jung 1953, para 11). I understand soul as that unlockable door residing within our body-self, our psychosomatic being, through which God (or whatever we put in place of God) can put a paw on us at any time.

Jung uses the term soul to denote a psychological faculty central to religious experience, and central to feeling oneself creatively alive and real. In conversation with Meister Eckhart, for example, Jung sees the soul as a definite complex, personifying contents of the unconscious (Jung 1921, paras 420-421): soul "is a function of relation between the subject and the inaccessible depths of the unconscious. The determining force (God) operating from these depths[1] is reflected by the soul, that is, it creates symbols and images" (Jung 1921, para 425). Soul shows in a willingness to respond, to be real and creatively alive in relation to others, to God, to self, even if in terror and dread (Ulanov A. and B. 1975, 91-92). Jung's view of the soul as "in an intermediate position" between conscious and unconscious makes me think of it as a two-way mirror, reflecting upwards to (ego) consciousness images of archetypal depths, and reflecting downwards to the unconscious what is going on in consciousness, especially the effects on our ego of the images reflected upwards from the unconscious. As Jung puts it, soul is "both receiver and transmitter" (ibid).

In the work of many mystics, soul dwells in depths of us inaccessible by rational intellect or ordinary words or dualisms of consciousness (Hollywood 1995, chapter 1). God as center of reality is also soul's 'breath of life' embodied in us, displaying the radical fact that ground of being is ground of us (though the relations

1. Note the distinction Jung makes between images of God and the Self archetype in the unconscious, though he just as often talks as if they are indistinguishable. For example, "the symbols of divinity coincide with those of the self: what, on the one side, appears as a psychological experience signifying psychic wholeness, expresses on the other side the idea of God (Jung 1958/1964, para 644). For example, "An archetype is an *image* ... a picture of something.... We find numberless images of God, but we cannot produce the original. There is no doubt in my mind that there is an original behind our images, but it is inaccessible" (Jung 1956-57/1976, para 1589).

of the two are very complicated and explained in diverse and conflicting ways). God is in the soul and the soul informs psyche about this groundedness (Jung 1950/1966, paras 139-140; Caputo 2011, 89-90; Ulanov 1984/2005, 280-283; Ulanov 1998/2004, 206; Ulanov 2008/2014, 181).

To see that psyche has trans-spatial and trans-temporal capacities and relation with soul, has effects in our clinical work. For example, a major consequence of trauma is loss of soul. Its mirroring function gets frozen or fragmented so that in addition to losing body flexibility and pleasure, we lose capacity to transcend "space-time barriers" in relation to the beyond (however we characterize it) and lose our capacity to live stably in space and time. Meaning goes missing; we cannot find it and fear it is destroyed forever. The ground beneath us cracks open. We cannot represent in word or even image what has happened to us. We have fallen out of being and suffer what Bion calls "nameless dread" as if surrounded by buzzing bees stinging us to death in a bombardment of unprocessed experiences "(Bion 1962, 96; Bion 1992, 1992, 45-46). We need the clinical relationship (or its equivalent) to perceive that this buzzing is reaching to communicate the unlived meaning of events, memories and panics that besiege us (Godsil 2014, p. 63).

Jung begins his odyssey in *The Red Book* to find the soul he discovers he had lost. Instead of turning his soul into a "scientific object" which he could study and have "many learned words for her ... the spirit of the depths forced me to speak to my soul, to call upon her as a living and self-existing being. I had to become aware that I had lost my soul" (Jung 2009, 232 and n 39).[2]

2. It is important to note the term spirit that is often used interchangeably with soul and in reference to psyche. The meanings of spirit are diverse. I understand it as referring to a collective phenomenon we may find in particular examples, such as a spiritual teaching, or Jung's "spirit of the times" and "spirit of the depths" in his *Red Book*. In that sense spirit is something in which we all dwell, whether we acknowledge it or not, in contrast to soul usually understood as being embodied in each of us. Yet spirit also refers to a superhuman force or power that is not subject to space and time and a bodily frame (Cross 1974, 1300), and exercises a certain autonomy designating energy, movement, breath; it will blow where it will and we do not know from where nor can we control where it will go. Spirit

Inaugural Images

We can see the soul's spark in what Jung calls our raw materials – the data, the stuff of our ongoing life despite trauma (Jung 1946/1954, para 400; see also Jung 1950/1966, para 140). Nestled there soul sparks (what he calls *scintillae*) exist, initiating what I see as inaugurating images that, even in dreadful suffering, persist (Jung 1963, paras 42, 45, 49, 50). Hence, despite the black hole of the dead mother of André Green's theory or the dead third of Samuel Gerson's theory, we are not dead yet, but, as Green puts it, "the love or life instincts – are responsible for this *growth,* this 'bud' of being" (Green 2000, 81; see also, Green 1993, 148-155; Gerson 2009, 1342, 1343). Jung says an individual's "traumatic complex brings about dissociation of the psyche". It shows its tremendous power and autonomy: "it pounces upon him like an enemy or a wild animal" (Jung 1928/1954, paras 266, 267). Yet it too is part of us and of any unity we may assemble; it is part of "a string of hard facts, which together make up the cross we all have to carry or the fate we ourselves are" (Jung 1946/1954, para 400).

Winnicott says is not interpretations, but new living experience with another that heals (Winnicott 1971, 117). I would also add that healing arises from such animated connection with heretofore missing parts of ourselves, and beyond ourselves with 'something more' that the soul knows about, and yearns to inhabit. When we respond to those inaugurating images a hum of meaning gets into play. A singing, a thinking, a perceiving, a nonpurposive purpose grows in us which we find instead of manufacture. We can spot those inaugurating images in theories we esteem – Winnicott's space of transition from which our symbols spring; Freud's space between the free-associating and the observing ego that allows freedom from instinct at the same time we channel its energies into life projects. In this space Kohut locates the cohesive self,

broods on the face of the deep; it may release us from crippling; it may be good or evil, and even part of God as the Holy Spirit (see Jung 1926/1960, para 602; see also Main 2007, 24-26; see also Ulanov 2000/2004). I will take up spirit again in chapter 6.

so elusive of definition but also central to living. Bion finds here the ultimate O, the emotional truth of the moment. Klein finds the mysterious triggering by our anxiety changing into guilt the instinctive response of our reparative efforts to make things better and to feel gratitude (see Ulanov 1992/2005, 32-33). Money-Kyrle finds the image of parental intercourse the supreme symbol of creating something good between self and other (See Meredith-Owen 2009, 459). Jung's image is the rhizome, growing in, of and through him of its own accord, including the damaged places, with its ownmost capacity to be and to flourish (Jaffé 1963, 4, 19, 20, 27), Jung's words, "the perennial rhizome beneath the earth ... the root matter is the mother of all things" remind me of the title of Celan's poem, "Radix Matrix" meaning "Root, Womb" (Jung 1956/1974, xxiv; Felstiner 2001, 175).

We each can give examples of inaugurating images in ourselves, and in our analysands, that if heeded, not only inspire faith in processes of psyche to communicate our distress (e.g. citing analysands, "I am disappearing down the bathtub drain"; "I am like an aborted mess") but also to salute emerging meaning (e.g. "the 'solid girl in me," "the dream instructs: I am to build a bridge"). Recovery from trauma includes spying soul's inaugurating images that plant a seed in us that we are to incarnate into a life. Jung calls such an image 'primordial' – not derived, not symptomatic of something else, but "a true symbol ... an expression for something real but unknown" and "intentionally kept secret ... hidden ... out of religious awe" (Jung 1950/1966, para 148). Such images open us to psychoid quality of unconscious processes and to something beyond psyche that looks at us, so to speak, from *its* point of view. Jung asks, "What if there were a living agency beyond our everyday human world ... a door that opens to the human world from a world beyond" to carry us "to a more than personal destiny?" (ibid.)

The psyche-soul question is, will we respond to these images, make something of them making something of us, for as Jung says: "Only what is really oneself has the power to heal" (Jung 1953/1966, para 258). I see these inaugural images as our nubs of being, as soul elements that generate original thinking and spontaneous emotion that fill us with hope for the precious smallness of our everyday lives in the large universe. These moments proffer a *coniunctio* of immediate child consciousness without preconceptions joining with adult reflection. Their conjunction imparts what Sedgwick, citing Proust, calls "a psychology of surprise and refreshment" (Sedgwick 2011, 4). Such a joining is lived but not known. As for the world – the *Anima Mundi,* the soul of the world – its transitions rely on each of us: "The individual who is not anchored in God can offer no resistance on his own resources to the physical and moral blandishments of the world" (Jung 1957/1964, para 511, see also 540).

If psyche/soul transcending space and time barriers truly matters, its effects show up in our clinical work. I cite three: experience of the psychoid quality of the unconscious in the transference/countertransference field as a place of healing even trauma in self and world; experience of two kinds of witnessing that help heal trauma; new experiences of transition, and of containers.

Two Sources of Healing

Remembering Jung saying in *The Red Book* that transformation happens in us, not in containers of religion nor in metaphysical figures of culture or politics outside ourselves, we shift to acknowledge a third kind of healing in Jung's corpus, in addition to the two with which we are more familiar.

Jung cites a first source of healing in our discovery that our particular problem, the core of trauma that befell us, the still powerful complex that dogs our days even after much work to become released from it, is part of human problems, not ours alone. Our complex mirrors a suffering afflicting our family, and, even wider, our particular culture and time in history. When this insight penetrates consciousness, instead of feeling trapped, we see we are harnessed into working on something that hurts the whole human family, both near – the intergenerational trauma – and afar – the culture of late 20th century, or the breakup of assumed cultural meaning in beginning of 21st century. We are healed or at least lightened from the burden of humiliation and isolation that our complex imposes on us (Jung 1984, 705, 22; Jung 1988, v. 2, 904-905; Jaffé 1963, 335; Ulanov 2013, 9).

We see the suffering that besieges us and our reparative efforts to relieve it compose our service to the whole. That insight confers meaning. Our efforts, however small in the largeness of life, are nonetheless valuable to the human family. Dignity re-forms. Like tellers at a specific window in the bank, we work on a particular problem of cash flow – flow of psychic libido: Where has it gone missing? Who has cheated? Stolen it? Run off with it? Injured it? Our efforts to solve these problems serve the health and wealth of the entire bank.

A second source of healing comes from Jung's project of making conscious the correspondence of truths in traditional symbols, especially religious and spiritual ones, with truths in images that arise in our own psyche. Such insight links us into age-old patterns of renewal and ritual that bespeak meaning (Jung 1953, para 20). Jung's intent is not to replace religion but to offer a renewed way into its truths, whatever the tradition, though he focused mainly on Christianity and pivotal views of God in the Hebrew Bible. Light exists, he says; analytical psychology can help us see the light by showing us the correspondence between the truth in religious symbols with the psychic images that appear in each of us. We feel a personal connection to age-old truths, those sighs too deep for words ("for all religions are therapies for the sorrows and disorders of the soul") (Jung 1945, 126). We come upon personal meaning of something revealed to us we did not know before, and feel released, indeed, even reborn (Jung 1953, paras 13-15).

Jung writes, "Many hundreds of patients have passed through my hands ... among all my patients in the second half of life – that is to say over thirty-five – there has not been one whose spoken problem in the last resort was not that of finding a religious outlook on life ... everyone fell ill because he had lost what the living religions of every age have given their followers, and none of them has really been healed who did not regain his religious outlook" (Jung 1933/1958, para 509).

For example, to see our painful being torn apart in opposite directions as in some way participating in the image of the crucified Christ, not knowing (according to Gospel of Mark) whether his death signals the triumph of evil, or that evil itself has been gathered up in God's plan, (according to Gospel of John) anchors our uncertainty as part of the God-man's life. It also shows, at least in one account of John's Gospel, that God does what we cannot do: God enters the suffering that evil causes and kills the death-dealing effects it inflicts.

Such a vision can have a revelatory effect: it communicates that somehow our suffering matters, is acknowledged, while also defeating its power to define our life. Indeed, in participating in that mystery another point of view inhabits us while being also beyond our comprehension. We pierce the boundaries of space and time.

Jung cites the ritual of The Round Dance in Apocryphal Acts of John, the dance of disciples around Christ at the center (Hennecke 1964, 227-232). Commenting on this rite, Jung observes that the one around whom all circle, shows a "symbol for the Deity, illustrating the wholeness of the God incarnate: the single point in the centre and the series of points constituting the circumference" (Jung 1954/1958, para 419). If our struggle with feeling pulled apart by death-dealing conflicts links with symbolic truth in this age-old ritual, instead of isolation from identifying oneself with a single point on the circumference, being drawn into identification with the one at the centre who chooses the suffering imposed on him, binds us together with him and with all others "of like mind" (ibid, para 419). What is thus created is "that ubiquitous *participation mystique* which is the unity of the many, the *one* man in all men" (ibid).

Connecting with that radical perspective liberates us from being designated by the complex or trauma that has captured us. The trauma is part of us; we are no longer engulfed in it. Through identification with the one as the nucleus in all persons, the one in the many, we find inner space to relate to the suffering that has fallen upon us and make it our own and win from that relation its life-saving meaning of the deity meeting us even in our suffering.

2. Psychoid Quality of the Unconscious, A Third Source of Healing

The Psychoid Quality of the Unconscious

A third source of healing, I suggest, springs from living experience of the psychoid quality of unconscious processes in a transference/countertransference field. Jung does not give a systematic presentation of what 'psychoid' means, which has to do, I believe, with its very nature. Contra its nature I will designate four main points to describe it.

To begin with, the term indicates a quality of unconscious process we undergo but cannot perceive directly or represent in word or image; it is unknown and unknowable. Jung writes, "It seems to me ... reasonable to take cognizance of the fact that there is not only a psychic but a psychoid unconscious" (Jung 1963, para 788): "a view which includes the psychoid factor in our description and knowledge of nature – that is, as *a priori* meaning or 'equivalence'" (Jung 1952/60, para 962). Jung finds the archetype is psychoid: it is not known straightforwardly but only derivatively through behavior, emotion, image the archetype generates: "a psyche that is identical in all individuals. It cannot be directly perceived or 'represented,' in contrast to the perceptible psychic phenomena, and on account of its 'irrepresentable' nature I have called it 'psychoid' (Jung 1952/1960, para 840; see also para 964; see also Jung 1946/1964, para 417).

Secondly, psychoid process and archetype manifest physically as well as psychically. In the psychoid aspect of the unconscious the physical and psychical are not two separate parallel tracks but two sides of the same thing, two sides of the same coin. Thus what we experience consciously as opposites – matter and mind, flesh and spirit, physical and psychical – link through a continuum of consciousness extending from instinctual to spiritual. Jung puts it simply: "Psychic processes therefore behave like a scale along which consciousness 'slides.' At one moment it finds itself in the vicinity of instinct and falls under its influence; at another, it slides along to the other end where spirit predominates" (Jung 1947/1960, para. 408; see also paras 368f, 380-381, 419-420; see also Jung 1952/1960, paras 840, 947, 962; see also Jung 1954/1976, para 1538; see also Addison 2009, 137, Addison 2011, 568).

Thirdly, Jung says experience of the psychoid and of synchronicity each give evidence of the existence of the other, and both open to what Jung calls (borrowing the term from alchemist Dorn) the *unus mundus*, the one world where familiar binary categories of ego no longer obtain (Jung 1963, paras 464-465, 766-770; see also Jung 1958a/1964, para 780: see also Main 2004, 20, 25-26, 51-52; Main 2007, 20, 52). In experiences of synchronicity opposite, noncausally related elements and/or events are thrown together; they coincide and impact us with tremendous sense of meaning, that meaningfulness exists objectively, independent of our constructions of it. We did not invent it (Jung 1952/1960, para 942). Yet this reality is present and presses for acknowledgment and the living of it. But living it means the ego is upended – psychic and physical boundaries come together simultaneously, as do those of inner/outer, past/present/future, here/there, even me/you, us/them. Those familiar categories of reference – space, time, substance, self, causality, dissolve (Jung 1946/1954, para 468, n. 8). We are in the land beyond the "space-time barriers." I think of experience of psychoid quality as consciousness of what is beyond consciousness; it can be lived, but not known or represented.

Fourthly, processes of the psychoid unconscious transgress all usual boundaries of clinical work. Because archetypes cannot be known or represented in word or image definitively, but known only "approximately ... they continually go beyond their frame of reference, an infringement to which I give the name 'transgressiveness,' because the archetypes are not found exclusively in the psychic sphere, but can occur just as much in circumstances that are not psychic (equivalence of an outward physical process with a psychic one)" (Jung 1952/1960, para 964; see also Monick 1987, 64-65). The transgressive quality of these processes in the analytic field shows itself by crossing of boundaries, breaking the usual ways of knowing, annulling usual reference points. Hence it is alarming and calls one to attention, and may also be felt as liberating in seeing a larger picture.[3]

Experience of the psychoid quality of the unconscious differs from (though may include and exceed) *participation mystique* constellated by the archetypal core of the patient's complex that often characterizes a beginning phase of analysis where an unconscious identity initially exists between analyst and analysand (Jung 1971, para 781; Jung 1946/1954, paras 375-376 and n. 27). In the psychoid experience each member of the analytical couple remains distinct, yet related by a sense of unity, being in something together, but not in a state of identity.

Experience of the psychoid quality of the unconscious also differs from the analyst having a sense of the analysand's content – rage, envy, despair – pushed into them and identified with them. The analysand does this projective identification unconsciously, but it holds a seed of future consciousness when the analysand comes into relation with this content and calls the content back into him or herself and relates to it consciously. In such projective identification the analyst can feel pushed around by this foreign

3. We may speculate about whether the psychoid quality of the unconscious is in play when ethical boundaries are trespassed, indeed violated. If so, I suggest that imposes on us real effort to understand the psychoid field lest our usual boundaries get swept away. Per usual, consciousness to the utmost is required.

element in oneself, though with more consciousness may feel as if carrying something temporarily for one's patient, as a proxy so to speak.

The Psychoid Field

In experience of the psychoid field in which analyst and analysand do the work of analysis, the analyst and analysand do not dwell in that initial state of identity, of being in the same soup bowl, because they remain distinctly themselves and because the image of the soup bowl is itself surpassed. Instead we feel united in something together, in a larger bowl, while aware the image of bowl does not translate accurately what is happening. We are together in looking at the material the analysand brings; we are together in being upended from all usual reference points in doing analysis; we are together in our ego-knowing being dissolved; we are together in each of us arriving at this experience by his or her own root images and path in life. We dwell together in something that is untranslatable by our language that both safeguards the secret and the hope to betray it into words (see Ricoeur 2004/2012, 28). We are not sure what is happening.

The relation between analyst and analysand becomes more equal – as two human beings each with their own paths to the content at hand whether it is traumatic or full of plenty. We are together in our separate ways in experiencing the psychoid field, coming to it, dwelling in it, how as humans we see and respond and deal with what is at hand.

But the loss of familiar markers and methods to conceive the material, make interpretations, use the inaugural image in the theory we love best to orient ourselves, may so unsettle us we are tempted to grasp at understanding in order to get a footing. But thereby we barricade against the *unus mundus* we have landed in, and not only miss that perception but also that our work together, even though upended, knows a second unity of joining in this one-world. We are together in our disarray and our experience together of the one-world.

The usual markers of what is going on fade, even what we now see as transition from our inhabiting a small bowl to a much larger one. There is at once no archimedian point outside the field from which to observe our experiencing of it (Jung 1947/1960, para. 421) and yet, at the same time, the coincidence of the *unus mundus* quality of a whole surround encompassing us functions as an archimedian point from which to register we are momentarily penetrated by a greater unity that is now the territory in which we find ourselves (see Brooke 2008, 592ff). In the analytic session coincidence of opposites occurs.

We may experience this one world quality as positive or negative. It can elicit panic – what is going on? We can feel frightened, amazed, liberated. In my experience boundaries become porous. Later, questions fly around. Are we operating on a subjective level? An objective level? An intersubjective level? A level that includes all of these, that exceeds symbolic interpretation? Are we lost? Found? Swept away? Delivered into environs that impress on us that individuation is not I, oneself, becoming whole, but each of us finding our place together in the wholeness of the whole? Trauma can take us there and working successfully with trauma will take us there. We may defend against this bigger terrain, block its symptoms of unraveling and thus leave chunks of our life, of our patient's life, of life's entirety unlinked and we fall into the gaps.

The analyst is rearranged, turned inside out, living in an experience that defies usual categories of understanding, leaving both analyst and analysand defeated and emancipated because ushered into something more. Evicted from our professional analytic position, we are tempted to try to reinstate our differentiations of me/you, inside/outside, causality, space, time, and resist a quality of reality pressing in on us. Yet we also feel disencumbered, freed for a livingness that bespeaks unity between analysand and analyst, *and* their unity with a surrounding whole reality.

Other Theorists, Mystics

We may experience both blanking one's mind, dwelling in a nowhere, yet also feel it not only as positive but joyous, a release into that big encircling that exceeds all our usual measurements, an all in all. This psychoid aspect of the unconscious might be likened to what other thinkers call the unrepressed unconscious comparing it with ideas of Matte Blanco (Carvallo 2014, 31), as a flooding of sensory meaningless beta elements from unrepresentable areas in Bion's theory (Godsil 2014, 61) or shown us by trauma (Cavalli 2014, 195), the unthinkable, unsymbolized, unconscious, the Self as comparable to Bion's 0 (Sullivan 2010, 54-56), the realm of the Real, though more positive than Lacan's emphasis.

I have been interested in a level, so to speak, of the unconscious describing it as beneath[4] the conflictual unconscious put forward by Freud and the unconscious of tumultuous affects designated by Jung. I have been mulling experiences of mystics as partaking of this unconscious quality Marguerite of Porete of the 14th century describes as bountiful living: "A country of peace so delicious that Truth calls it glorious food," where one is "very free and unencumbered from all things." She speaks of her relation to this country in personal terms of connection to its author whom she calls "'the Ravishing most High' who overtakes me and joins me to the marrow of divine love in whom I am melted" recalling Jung saying in *The Red Book* he was 'smelted' anew (Porete in Babinsky 1993, 135-6; Jung 2009, 247).

The mystics show a sturdiness to move into the fullness of the whole world, the *unus mundus,* despite wretched suffering of condemnation, exile, even death. Nonetheless, we see in their writings their loving experience of chaos as plenty, abundance, recalling what Fordham said so long ago, "the primary self ... [is]

4. I think of Mephistopheles in Goethe's *Faust* when saying to Faust to descend to The Mothers (of the deep unconscious), "Down you go, then. I might equally say: Up you go. It's all the same. Escape the created world and enter the world of forms.... You'll see it all as drifting clouds." (cited in Edinger 1990, 55).

... indestructible (Fordham 1974 also cited by Godsil 2014, 59). Reading that, I remembered a dream a student gave me decades ago with permission to cite, saying it proved a pivotal turning point in her life attacked by mental illness. The dream showed her small Volkswagon car being smashed by cosmic and personal forces from all sides and it did not break! It did not split apart, but survived in the small green intactness of its cardom.

Healing Potential of the Psychoid Field

The point I am making is that touching the psychoid realm can feel like losing your mind as well as being ushered into bounty, amplitude, full measure, solidity, that no matter how great the damage through trauma these unconscious processes go on, there to be accessed, and people do access them and know joy and gratitude. I think of an analysand who at seventy allows herself to become fully conscious of the aloneness, sadness, unshed tears of a lifetime of the unmothered small girl part of her. She is astonished and grief-struck how decades of her life feel shaped, indeed dominated, by this lost part, always near but never fully lived. It has been present in depression, isolation, unsuccessful efforts to succeed in the world, and in blocked realization of spiritual efforts to give herself to God. She resists swamping regret and harsh inner scolding for 'a wasted life,' reaching instead to feel the small girl's sadness and anger at being disregarded, not listened to, whose enthusiasm for living has been rejected. She is amazed and overcome that the unshed tears pour out when connecting to this child part who is ready for joy, still, now. Sorrow and joyousness mix together and she feels alive in a depth of feeling not accessible before – of anger, enthusiasm for adventures, mourning, sexual and spiritual openings. Trauma though not removed, can be depotentiated so that it no longer defines us.

A living experience with another in the psychoid quality of the unconscious brings into consciousness alive connection of our tiny individual self, so big in importance to us, with the hugeness of the whole. They link together, they coincide in body and mind, in psyche and soul, matter and energy. One feels possible because in touch with meaningfulness that exists independently. We feel we matter, know to what we belong and what we can contribute. Such an experience is a spiritual event felt in the ordinary physical material realm.

This psychoid quality of unconscious processes is not the result of repression but is there anyway, beneath, before repression. This is important to grasp because in working with trauma wounds, both physical and mental, of soul and psyche, it suggests that beneath trauma is another level of unconscious processes going on. Might we ask in Jung's concepts, the ego suffers the shattering of trauma but does the Self ? Or another way to put it, beneath the pain to and damage of a child of an absent mother, there still exist mothering aspects of psyche that can be found and lived, an environing sense of matrix the child may find and create. Or underneath the damage inflicted by sexual violation, the body-psyche sexual instinct is there humming, and may be reached, so that this gift of pleasure may still be available.

To use Jung's phrases, *coincidentia oppositorum* – the struggling, conflicting elements in us – become *complexio oppositorum* – a gathered bundle of those elements in a complicated assembly that sticks together though not yet a fully working whole. Jung writes, "The psychoid nature of the archetype contains very much more than can be included in a psychological explanation. It points to the sphere of the *unus mundus*, the unitary world.... Although the first step in the cognitive process is to discriminate and divide, at the second step it will unite what has been divided, and an explanation will be satisfactory only when it achieves a synthesis" (Jung 1958/1964, para 851). What gets differentiated (analyzed) and then brought together (synthesized) is the you and I of the analytic couple, and the two of us with the larger unity of one world, in the two separate personal routes to this moment of great meaning, and the linking of this meaning to meaningfulness that exists.

Blooming

The evolving may go further into Jung's notion of *coniunctio oppositorum*. The assembly of conflicting elements changes further into the parts mutually penetrating that yields a completely different joining, as if the problem itself has changed into a new possibility. Further, this new capacity, brimming with energy, enlivens us at a deep level, all the way down, and opens to a bigger perspective. We are changed by moments of aperture to the one wholeness of the whole (*unus mundus*). Such experience of "ecstatic transcendence" is known to mystics, artists, lovers, sages, and anyone living creatively" (Monick 1987, 65). Our ego becomes the sous-chef, and knows it. Experience of the psychoid level of the unconscious plants a seed of the larger circumference of reality.

The seed may grow into steady awareness that precious ego judgments, principles, even its woundedness have a place in something more, a greater whole, a unity of everything in which we play an important part. That living experience brings healing of deepest madness. Does madness evaporate? Not usually, but it could. Madness as our persistent complex is disempowered to run the show, to be the chef in charge. Our madness and the horrors of destructiveness that may come from it are part of the whole, and with its own place. The seed the psychoid plants shows its bloom and something in us knows this; the more it roots us, the more it changes our perspective *sub specie aeternitatis*. Emily Dickinson got it in her poem "Bloom – is Result – to meet a Flower" (Dickinson in Johnson 1960, 482); see these last two stanzas:

> To pack the Bud – oppose the Worm –
> Obtain its right of Dew –
> Adjust the Heat--elude the Wind –
> Escape the prowling Bee
>
> Great Nature not to disappoint
> Awaiting Her that Day –
> To be a Flower, is profound
> Responsibility –

To miss this experience, never to feel in touch with the psychoid seed and *unus mundus* blooming, that we are linked within meaningfulness, that meaning matters, may account for rageful killing of others by mass shooters in staging the killing of themselves. One's despairing outrage of never finding where one fits in, seeing others as those who do fit in and hence exclude oneself, turns one vengeful, determined to eradicate as many others as possible (hence the use of automatic guns) before killing oneself, or getting the police to do it.

Experience of the psychoid level of the unconscious plants a seed of the larger circumference of reality. At the psychoid level all is mixed in with all else; at the *unus mundus* level, the opposites are differentiated and surpassed in the entirety of interdependence of reality. It is a wholeness as if disclosed to us, revealed, and we are able to open to it: a mutual opening in that sense.

Scraps

These apertures are inaugurated not by logic or learning literal steps or stages of progression, but by chance, by accidents, by scraps of insight, a body-felt hunch. (Ulanov 2014, 226f, 231-233). We get nudges, we get a whiff [5], hear a whisper, spot a slight pointer. In one glance we embrace the simultaneity of our idiosyncratic particularity with another's and with the human community that transpires time, over past and into future. Having spyed the whole, we pierce "time and space barriers" and sing along with our neighbor Ella Fitzgerald or put our question to Augustine. We recall our friend's simple act of kindness, sometimes sight Buddha appearing in our children, their significance stretching from present to all time in the future. We feel excitement for the future healing of cancer in a present researcher's insight to investigate not the cancer cell, but the system in which the cancer

5. Jung writes, "libido, which is not only creative and procreative, but possesses ... a strong power to 'smell the right place,' almost as if it were a live creature with an independent life of its own" (Jung 1956/1974, para 182).

cell acts like a gangster mugging other cells. Beginning evidence indicates changing the environment of a cancer cell to remove its aggravating agents stimulates a cancer cell to develop as part of community of normal cells. The really bigger soup bowl brings healing agents from all sides that we in our usual smaller bowl can hardly imagine.

Hence I emphasize the importance of the analyst reflecting on the real, what it is to each of us, for that deep level shapes how we listen and what we can hear. Alert to what frightens us to death and what flickers like a *scintilla* of a completely other way of viewing existence, we see that may be going on right there in our office between us and our analysand. A revolution may be occurring.

Meaning and Its Paradox

Psychoid experience gives us a sense of meaningfulness that exists objectively, independent of our constructs of it; we do not produce it. It shows itself. Experiences of synchronicity throw together noncausally related things that impact us with this objective meaning. Yet we do not know this objective meaning unless we subjectively register its impact.

So right away our usual categories of understanding are disrupted, disordered. Objective self-subsistent meaning is real when we register it subjectively. The objectiveness of it comes through coincidence of opposites falling together in a way that deeply impresses us subjectively with meaningfulness – pointing, revealing something greater, a break-through. But the meaning does not exist for us unless we get it in the terms of the most subjective details, the scraps of our personal lives, peculiar to us. Intellectual rational understanding gives way to paradoxical understanding – the objective exists because of the subjective, its realness is admitted through the subjective idiosyncratic scraps peculiar to us. Yet the anchoring of our subjective lives gains real significance through registering objective meaning existing independent of us. The subjective exists because of the objective, and vice versa.

Among Jungian analysts there is controversy and discussion of this meaningfulness and where and how it exists, Does it exist objectively, like a 21st century version of God of Middle Ages, or does this meaning arise from our human capacity of meaning making (See Bright 2014, 85; see Colman 2011, 477, 488)? My view is we need both views: to see the phenomenon of synchronicity and the psychoid as indicating meaning that exists outside us, and that we have a hand in its making. I say this for two reasons. The first, as I said above, we must respond to the impact of meaningfulness showing itself for the meaning to register in us as real. Without our personal and peculiar response, whatever meaning is there does not enter our lives, and we do not open to it. For objective, independent meaning to occur as real to us we must respond to it. Its objectivity lies within our subjectivity, so to speak. Yet, secondly, to repeat, of course our process of meaning-making in symbol formation helps shape the meaning that shows itself. The degree to which we gather associative responses – personal, cultural, archetypal – emerges in relation to what appears from its objective self-determining existence exterior to us. Our subjectivity lies within its objectivity. In the moment of experience, full of fear, awe, soul response, whether meaningfulness is objective or subjective is not the question.

But that question does come, because we want to know, on reflection at least if not in the moment, is this madness, as Mohammed thought when he heard voices and feared for his sanity? Or is this truth and directed at me, that I must attend, ponder, even obey? We need to know the status, so to speak, of this otherness addressing me and coming into my actual living: is it true or did I make it up? The ethical consequences hang on how we answer those questions. Without the counsel of his wife and his uncle, Mohammed might not have heeded the voices that spoke to and through him into the Koran.

The Ubiquity and the Aura of the Psychoid

I would add that psychoid experience exists everywhere, not only in transference/countertransference field of analysis. We notice it there, drag it into representation, dialogue. But its seed of our experience of objective meaning felt subjectively, of uniting with an other from our own route of access through the path of our individual lives, and our uniting with a greater unity of reality so we partake of the all in all in the particularity of our lives, those many bits create an aura of possibility. Something is in being and we come to see it, know it. We feel the numinous here and now, a moment of great importance, an aura that is a diffusion or emanation of atmosphere, mood, tone, even an engendering sound that exists around us and among us in the reality that circumferences all of us.

Writing this I hear again the words of Nancy whose dying I wrote about in *The Wizards' Gate: Picturing Consciousness* (1994). In the midst of outrage and sorrow at her life cut short by illness, when still able to form words, though near the end, when looking at all the pictures she drew of her struggle to meet death coming to meet her, now mounted together on the wall facing her, she said, "This is worth it. It's all been worth it." The psychoid level bespeaks possibility no matter the circumstances. I also remember my late husband's words, when flesh and spirit meet, each becomes more of itself.

As a coda I must note that trying to write about the psychoid, indeed touching it in any way, constellates being in its field. Again coincidence strikes: one's strenuous, repeated and protracted efforts to present the psychoid quality of the unconscious in word and image, is thrown together with the boundless, borderless nature of the psychoid field. Time dissolves, spatial limits disappear. One discovers one has been at the task 4-5 hours with no sense of passing time nor definitions of body in space. It is like trying to write water but instead feeling taken under the waves and out to sea; it is like trying to write air, and instead wafted up into currents above the earth and delineations of human life within time and space. There are side-effects to piercing space-time barriers, and no guarantee one makes anything clear. Yet, and yet, there hovers around such unhinging a spaciousness and a beyond-timeness that conveys freedom from constraints, as if ushered into where one belongs and contributes to the wholeness of the whole and is full of gladness to do so.

3. Examples of Psychoid Quality of Unconscious

Because the psychoid opens into a vast area, specific examples may help to illustrate ways it comes upon us. I list five, all of which show its possible healing effect. The first from transference/countertransference field in analysis has to do with trauma; the second to do with self inflicted violence; the third with traumatic wound to society; the fourth a happening between colleagues that touched a long ago grave loss, the fifth a man's experience with bees.

Example 1: Murder

My analysand is telling a dream of a psychopathic killer out to get her and wondering if such cold-bloodedness lives in her. On the way to developing this theme she mentions in passing, in brief condensed form, that when she was six and her brother four, her mother cut their wrists when they were sleeping. She awoke from the 'pinch' on her wrist and heard her brother screaming. That called others to the rescue.

I felt complete shock. This offhand mention of something so traumatic was news to me. My patient clearly assumed I knew this. Did I? I asked myself. Had I known and forgotten this? How could I have forgotten something so vital, so horrific? Did I have notes on this and if so, where were they? Doubt, confusion, a kind of blankness overcame me and I flashed on my patient often saying she felt overcome by blankness. She would say I do not know what to do, I just feel blank. I am too confused and unfocused even to be in a painful state; it can go on for hours. I felt in my present blankness a crossing of time to the distant past of her six year old self in her bed of her childhood home here in the office session, and into the hours of blankness in her present home, let alone my feeling of being nowhere clearly.

I felt invalid – what is wrong with me as an analyst to be so careless not to be remembering something so terrorizing! Had I been told, or had I never been told? Had this happened or was it now happening for this first telling?

My analysand felt something similar – confusion, doubt, what was happening? Had she told me before? Why did she think I already knew? Did I already know of this murderous attempt and had forgotten it? Had it really happened? Had she forgotten it and how could she forget it? Did she make it up? My analysand asked herself what was wrong with her not to know the status of this decisive event.

That conviction 'there is something wrong with me' was the name of her central complex and here it was in the middle of this upending session when the two of us landed in a field of no markers, no reference points, no explanation for what was going on in what we were doing. This conviction of being fatally flawed, was the madness that held her hostage. When she told me at the very beginning of her analysis, 'I have always felt there is something wrong with me,' I knew something had happened to her that inscribed that meaning of being marred, blameworthy. That certainty repeated whenever misunderstandings or conflicts came up in daily life, or when lack of hope to be able to live peaceably and with happiness transpired. She was the reason: there is something wrong with me.

We were both in the same emotional state but got there by our individual routes. I was asking what was wrong with me as an analyst not to remember, to know, this decisive trauma in my analysand's life. But it was not like a *participation mystique* where the two are in state of identity, an *a priori* oneness of subject and object that can mark the beginning of an analysis (Jung 1921/1971 para 781, Jung 1946/1954, paras 375-376), nor was this a scene of projective identification where something unconscious in the analysand is projected into the analyst and pushes her around to display, at least inwardly, the tone or content or emotion of that part of the patient who remains unconscious of it.

We were distinct reaching this state of crossing time, place, blanking of (ego) mind. I was experiencing my own version of what my patient suffered. I arrived on my own, not from my analysand pushing me there. I joined from my own experiences of death-dealing attacks and then blaming myself as if something wrong me with me was their cause. We dwelt together, each from her own path in the human problem of murderous assaults and blaming ourselves, not identical experiences but shared focus on a problem afflicting the entire human family.

In this event between us revealing her mother's attack on her children I dimly discerned a causality between her conviction something is wrong with me and this trauma. But causality faded, dissolved in the evocation in me coming to trauma of being killed from my own experiences of invalidation – what is wrong with me. I felt all those ways of not feeling right in myself, a lack, default, deficit. I felt evicted from the role of analyst, not knowing what is going on, turned inside out, unsettled in my symbolic grasp of what was happening, feeling both of us in confusion yet ushered into something more.

We stayed put looking at the horror of the event of a mother killing her children, and the horror of losing our minds. We sat in that together in a sort of unity, but not a fusion or merger. What emerged was some reality pressing into us, a quality of reality that bespeaks a unity of us with it, joining with a surrounding entire reality. These are not causal connections but simultaneities, synchronistic coincidences gathering everything up into a larger whole.

We discussed this happening in subsequent sessions, crossing time and space – present in my office with time past in her childhood bedroom decades before – and even into time future feeling this was heading somewhere as yet unknown. We inhabited deep insecurity about our capacity to know truth, to perform our respective roles as analyst-analysand.

Somehow I knew not to press for every detail of the murderous episode but to rest content with what was telling itself – the disjointed memories, the mental wounds mixed with physical sensations in her wrist and arm that would sometimes ache now in the session, like two sides of the same event she relayed. To press for every detail of trauma event seems perverted to me, turning the main purpose of reaching speech into pernicious curiosity. Also emotional memories of such inflicted pain stir up monstrous rage at being so intruded upon. Great tact is required when such pain opens up (Davoine and Jean-Max Gaudilliere 2004, 146, 256).

Through confusion and self-doubt we bridged the space of then and now with such questions as, how could this be happening? Analysts are meant to keep such major acts in mind; mothers are not meant to kill their children; trauma victims are not meant to think they are the guilty ones for a bad act.

Like a leitmotif we dipped in and out of this theme until another startling event occurred just before summer break in our work. She sent me a copy she made of a newspaper clipping she found by chance in a book while sorting books to give away. In bald, succinct, reportorial style two paragraphs stated the crime, arrest, and imminent hospitalization of her mother, by name, for "cutting her children." This 'factual' summary retrieved both my analysand and me from the brink of confusion and doubt. The newspaper established the externality of this event – it did happen; she did not make it up; she did not cause it. The scar on her wrist marked a dreadful trauma. She did not make a mountain out of a molehill. For me, I had not been told until that day; I had not forgotten it nor lost my notes. My patient thinking I knew it attested to her being in the work, that here the thing would be known, secrets told, and an emotional connection forged.

I repeated in miniature, however, the cycle of confusion and doubt by temporarily not finding the copy of the newspaper clipping – did I receive it? How could I lose something so important?

What kind of analyst am I? I felt relieved finding it in my folder of notes and both my patient and I felt relief to secure facts differentiated from our internal experience.

The newspaper clipping safely returned us to the world of what Jung calls personality number 1 of everyday reality in contrast to personality number 2 which was the psychoid field between us that pierced space and time, and with its porous boundaries revealed an emotional truth of the two of us as sister humans facing and working on the terrible problem of destructiveness in human life. As my patient said, it is important to me to be clear what is inside and what is outside me.

Yet she also said, and I understood it as a healing from psychoid experience, that because she saw I could feel unmoored as did she, both of us together moved beyond space-time markers to something bigger, both together doubting what had happened and our ability to know it, both evicted and freed from conventional roles of analyst/analysand while in them still, living something utterly real pressing beyond usual space-time barriers, in it together, and linked to a bigger unity, all that made her know our work was real, trustworthy. She could trust me; she could trust herself; she could trust our work. I saw in this psychoid field she had, I had, we had together, a new living experience.

This new living experience exerted healing effects on my analysand's major complex of 'something is wrong with me'. In the following months a space was emerging between that conviction and her ownmost self. That space keeps expanding. That complex, still bedeviling, no longer holds her hostage.

An example that gives evidence of a growing distinction between her self and the complex's conviction, was blatant and even with a brush of humor, though she was deadly serious in the emotion. She had brought some photos to show me of herself as small girl standing with her mother and father and some of her siblings. I got up from my chair and went over to where she was seated to see them. She said, when you plopped down in the chair next to mine I thought you were going to strangle me. There it was – the root of the complex – if my own mother would kill me there must be something really wrong with me. But to say it so simply and with a whisper of humor – we both smiled – gave evidence of a space opening up between a long held assumption of her wrongness and where it came from, and her own actual self. She and I were having a new living experience of looking at something together and of a space opening between her and the complex.

This space slowly enlarges. The condition of being ruled by the complex slowly changes into a symptom that can be noticed as a trigger to set off engulfment by the complex. Here it is again. Symptom slowly gathers and deepens into symbol, pointing to what kidnapped her through her personal material and extending into archetypal force of human experience of destructiveness. Back and forth we transit, reaching perception that through our trauma we work on an element of human existing – both the horribly destructive and also what can come to release and heal all that energy to thrive in living.

Example 2: Violence

A second example. A patient worked hard to assimilate the trauma of suicide of a beloved other on whom he depended in his early life. Now a middle-aged man, he fell apart with telephone news that a childhood friend tried to hack off his head with a big kitchen knife. He lived. My patient was disoriented. He knew about suicide in its many permutations and he felt all right in himself about his own past experience and working through it. But he was devastated by the violence and suffering of his childhood friend. He felt he suffered what his friend suffered – destructiveness made manifest – not as if he relived the ruin of the earlier suicide in his own life, but that he was in the grip of his friend's ferocious brutality, that such destructiveness existed and could lay waste to people.

My patient called me at night, pouring forth the event and his being taken down into his friend's death spell. I could feel this grip of destructiveness, myself in it too, even on the phone in my kitchen. This may remind us of the primary identity that begins transference/countertransference of archetypal constellation pulling us in. But it is not the same; here we are distinct, not identical. It is different from *participation mystique,* perhaps more accurately, includes and surpasses it. This is akin to perception we are all in life together, encircling us. What demolishes the other demolishes me, indeed, all of us, and we each experience our versions of it. Saying his friend is mentally ill, which he is, does not relieve it. That is our feeble effort to erect distinctions to protect our self. This savagery lives in the human family and its problem with annihilating forces is our problem. We hope not to be there until we are strong enough not to be broken by it.

It is as if we three crossed time and space barriers – his friend in hospital undergoing multiple surgeries, my patient in his home and me in my kitchen, all together in the current of destructiveness let loose against the self, to kill it. All of us are now to work on what to do with this barbarity, how to guard against its contagion, live in the face of its erupting. We feel how interdependent we are. We work for the same bank; the problems you have afflict me; my problems break out against you. We catch sight of our living in an encompassing world we share across the ages. That also includes the joyousness of your solutions spilling over to me, or my scrap of courage emboldens you to speak from your heart in public meeting at a crucial moment.

Evidence of our interdependence shows in the horrifying consequences when our mutual dependence breaks down and the most vulnerable among us, because least protected by healthy defenses,[6] can think to do the unthinkable, like the German pilot who plotted to murder 150 people in his act of suicide by crashing his plane into a mountain, or the American youth who decided to shoot small children in a Connecticut school as he staged being murdered by the rescuing police.

6. Winnicott distinguishes between healthy and reactive defenses. Healthy defenses against our impulses are flexible, adaptive to changing needs and circumstances. Reactive defenses are rigid and made to deal with someone else's hate, instead of one's own. (Winnicott, D. W. 1969/1989, 249).

Example 3: Psychoid Experience in Social Life

This example shows the social side of what gets eclipsed from consciousness, cut out of social history, just as traumatic events get banished from personal narrative with the same dire consequences of dragging deadness into aliveness, or worse, by burying something alive. These instances do not get recognized in tales of family lore, or in records of a town's past, or in a nation's textbooks of its history, but nonetheless exist and press to get into awareness, and usher us into psychoid quality of the unconscious as they emerge. They are present but not known, not shared and talked over among us, not admitted into our social life to be repaired, mourned, healed.[7] To reach them, which happens in an unexpected psychoid field that emerges between people, is to feel that disordering of the world of personality number 1 to reach another realm of truth that has been denied and lives in hiding.

My analysand worked hard to recover to his awareness missing pieces of himself hiding in flat line moods, and to address his major fear that he would not show up for the rest of his life. He uncovered important bits that expanded his capacity to reach tremendous human feelings without, as Winnicott would say, "excessive organization of defenses against anxiety" (Winnicott 1988, 50).

Along these lines he mulled over his life in the South of the United States, to which he was deeply attached. Dreams brought images of his grandparents and great grandparents, and with a favorite aunt he talked over the lives of these people who were her parents and grandparents. He pressed for details of their lives and

7. Lecturing in Australia In September 2014, I was greatly impressed by the public mourning of citizens' past segregation and abuse of aboriginal people. There are moving accounts in museums of suffering inflicted and borne, and people bring up their guilt for it in conversation. In museums of modern art there are exhibits of spectacular contemporary paintings by aboriginal artists. However, it was also announced on BBC News February 15, 2017, that the government had failed to meet four of its five goals to support and improve the lives of the aboriginal population. Redoubling of effort to do so was in order.

learned, yes, of course they were landowners, not plantations, but land of some acres. Pressing further about how they farmed their land, he discovered from his aunt they had help. What kind of help? Well, African-American helpers, then called Negroes, she said. Then he said to his aunt, you mean slaves. A long silence ensued, he said, holding him and his aunt. The word 'slaves' sunk in and in. With tears in her eyes his aunt said, we didn't call them that then. His tears met hers, and I found myself moved by this recounting, drawn into the wound with which, I believe, we Americans as a nation still have not come to full terms; it still inflicts hurt of very deep shame and rage. So my patient, his aunt, and I traversed time and space, our separate lives, then/now, south/north, they two, we two, and all three of us drawn into that realm of wound, both physical and psychical, covered up and now exposed, of crushing peoples' freedom to be subjects in their own right with rights over their lives.

My patient went on saying his aunt described how attached the family and the helpers were, especially this or that one in particular who became friends or were educated with the family's children, with stories of mutual giving that supported the idea of shared affection. But then, she said, when emancipation came, the helpers left. They just left. They were discovered gone one morning. No goodbyes, no ceremonies of leave-taking. That goneness sobered the enchantment of affection, countered the notion of happy togetherness. The missing side of that relationship entered history, bringing disorientation, sorrow, and recognition into our consulting room. It was as if no years intervened, as if we now granted living space to people long dead, crowding in with his aunt, all the helpers whose necessity for free standing subjectness trumped affection.

Example 4: Psychoid Experience in Everyday Life

An example of psychoid experience in everyday life occurred by chance between me and a colleague and shows that such events come in many forms. I asked how her summer was and she answered that the month of August was a hard one always as it marked the anniversary of her mother's death when she was an eight-year old girl. This was news to me. She had been shuffled among relatives for several months while her mother was sick, not being told her mother was dying, nor that she then did die. So loss and loss of the experience of loss haunted her.

Every August she made efforts to honor the mother she missed having and could hardly remember, feeling again the upheaval and bewilderment around her illness and death. She said Kaddish for her mother; she went to see art because she had been told her mother liked art. But it was clear she felt miserable now and these gestures did not relieve her heartache. I don't know what made me say this or hit upon precisely this. The usual courteous constraints against barging into another's suffering seemed to fade. I felt fleeting bits of abandonment and death-dealing events stir me, as if I was in the realm of bafflement about where was mother and what happened and how could this happen that no one seemed to notice this small girl. I said just what arrived, I know not from where; it spoke from that knowing that we do not know. "But what will you be doing for the eight-year-old girl who lost her mother and had been left in the dark about it until her mother was long dead? What can you be doing to comfort her and receive her pain?" And some such sentences. My colleague's eyes opened wider and tears filled them. "You have done for the mother, honored her," I said. "Reach to the small girl, do for her, honor her."

All four of us – my colleague and I, the small girl and her mother, and more, myself as a small girl with my colleague's small girl, my experiences of mother-loss and hers, all separate and distinct – seemed to join in a unity across time and space barriers of past now present, loss now found, crossing life and death, mourning and discovery, present misery extending into future pleasures to bring solace to the eight-year old girl. I soon departed and my colleague stood up and with solemnity put her hands in prayer position and bowed. I felt the small girl being honored right there in the room and I also bowed in her honor.

Jung goes so far as to say our problems may also be God's problems. Working on them, suffering them, connects us to the center deep inside us and far outside us – what the orthodox Christians call "The Existing One." That brings great joy, spilling over to each other.

It may be joyous too to experience this psychoid quality of unconscious. We fall into it everywhere, always there. And can feel the gladness that two people can meet in a day unexpectedly and feel that plenty, there, ready to soften heartbreak, plenty available to reunite with a long-missing part, as if all of us together, unite with something more that pervades us.

Example 5: A Man's Experience

Is the psychoid known only in clinical relationship? No, of course not. After lecturing on the psychoid in Australia, a man told me he used to keep beehives. He described standing in their midst without protective clothing with the bees all over his body and around him. I perceived he received in this bodily way deep connectedness to the real. He said, "I loved my bees" (see also Baring and Cashford 1993, 118-120).

4. Mending Trauma

Recognizing the level of psychoid experience as existing, coming to consciousness many ways many different times, what effects does that have for our clinical work? It helps mend trauma.

Mending

Any of us touched by trauma, our own and those of our analysands, know the awful erasure of mind it leaves in its wake, like Andre Green's black hole of the missing mother that attracts all else into its no-thingness. For example, lacking a container smashed by trauma of dramatic loss as in collective attack in holocaust of a whole people, or succumbing to blank mind on a personal level because we never had a maternal container to lose, we get crazed symptoms. We compulsively lose containers necessary for living – dropping our passport in its holder on the airport floor, or leaving money in its wallet in the taxi, or our purse in the grocery cart as we drive away, having loaded the bags of food in our car. Or we drop out of the time-space where we are, staring off into nowhere, losing touch with the event or gathering of people of which we tried to be a part. Such repeated behavior happens outside our consciousness, unrepresented in thought or word so we cannot gain the hidden meaning that dominates our actions with its repetitions.

Jung's notion of the prospective function of the symbol, here reduced to the repetitive symptom, if patiently looked into, dragging into awareness how invalid such repetitions make us feel, may slowly move toward mending trauma. I do not say reversing trauma or getting rid of it for its ruin dents us. Mending means finding ways to house it, no longer predetermined by its impact, but nonetheless bearing its weight.

What we get instead is consciousness weighed down by hurt from injury, rage and sorrow over what happened and goes on happening because we cannot bear it into knowledge and mourn it. What is denied yet present shows itself in imperative actions, hallucinations, strange objects, even delusions that appear to us and others as completely mad, but that also seek to break through into communication of what is buried alive in us. Such bizarre habits strip meaning from these potential bulletins. We need to find a link to their hidden news, helping us to recognize and represent what happened (Godsil 2014, 70; Cavalli 2014, 209).

The psychoid level of experience, if possible to bear, can weaken barriers against seeing into the symptoms of loss of soul and world at the center of trauma that felled us. The psychoid experience of the all in all, of time travel into past blows and present numbness, of the damaging other and the wrecked self, of the ownmost self still able to be found and lived, of distinct parts all jumbled together now at once, can loosen rigid denials. The symptom may move, slowly, from entrapping us to disclosing its hidden meaning if we can respond to its message. Loss of valuable containers like a purse or a passport holder or the gathering of friends now bespeak the container we never had to lose or the one we had and lost forever by injury by an other's madness. Those losses kept us stuck, like a person in a foreign country without papers to pass freely into the world of shared existence with others, or with a missing purse that had the names and numbers of an identity supporting us existing as particular subjects, or with absence that kidnaps us from community with others.

We get close to the blankness, the black hole, the gap between functioning and not being fully alive and slowly the trauma may begin to find mendings. We can then know it and feel its dreadful hold, but not be defined by it. It exists in us, indeed we carry it, but we no longer live hostage to its domination (Atwood 2014; Godsil 2014, 60-61).

We drag into consciousness trauma and its effects of loss of the 'good object' inside, leaving the empty space of the 'dead mother,' and loss of capacity to create something with another, what Samuel Gerson calls the 'dead third.' Kimmel, reviewing this idea, says it is "an internalized world of inner deadness ... that guards against the unbearable" (Gerson 2009 and Kimmel 2011, 571; see also Ogden 2001, 11-13, 19-20; see also Ulanov 2007, 589-592).

Flashbacks

One of the worst effects of trauma is flashbacks. There we are once again back to Square 1 as if the trauma inflicts its blow for the first time. Utterly discouraged, we feel all our work on it has gotten us nowhere; we still live in devastation. We have learned nothing, grown nothing. And yet. Clinical work has shown me another way to understand such flashbacks. We did go 'forward;' now we go 'backward.' But in the psychoid field those spatial boundaries recede, dissipate. We are curiously both forward and backward at once – a coinciding of opposite constructs with a piercing of their meanings with some greater meaning that emerges as questions: where is this heading? To what purpose aims this simultaneity of opposite things thrown together?

Here is a possibility. Because of the work we have done and the strength we have grown in relation to this trauma, we are taken back and down again to the nadir of injury, loss, rage, to scoop up the next layer of the affliction, to work now on this deeper level, to assimilate it and to differentiate from it. Our previous work on earlier levels of hurt increases our capacity to hear more acutely the communication attempted in the mandatory, repetitive symptoms. The primal trauma keeps replaying itself in one form or another. For example, if loss is trauma's central theme, it is a loss that needs to be finally and fully found and felt, and will not leave one alone until this occurs.

But now on the basis of work we have already done in relation to trauma, we experience at once, not in sequence but in simultaneity in the present, a past happening and a future opening, a more profound level of suffering and greater space from it through working on it. At the same time we are constructing images and meanings of causality – because we are stronger emotionally and with greater understanding – we can tackle the next level of hurt, especially in a psychoid realm where all causal connections evanesce. We reconstitute spatial and temporal dimensions and categories of causality and self while coinciding with the psychoid quality of surpassing all those familiar reference points, falling out of them, liberated from them. They do not hold but yield a sense of being in a bigger bowl or sustaining process, with meaning of something more impressing itself toward us, indeed beyond what we have known. We feel the whole jumble of hurt and healing, rage and understanding, devastation and commitment to work on our piece of the puzzle of human destructiveness and joy. We spot the whole venture and also the far side of its initiation from another source (Porete's Source of source) that feels near in eliciting our desire to contribute to this venture.

How to relate to all this without going under the wave and out to sea? The ego is doing the relating; the archetypal dimension is the force of the wave; the out to sea is beyond archetypal structures – the reality girdling all, or, the God beyond the archetypal god if speaking in religious/spiritual terms.

Trauma pushes us to do this work in order to survive. Do we want to say, ah, good comes from evil, trauma has purpose of effecting this greater vision and our inhabiting of what it depicts? No. We do not want to say that. I do not. Pain hurts. And pain is not the exclusive route. We can reach to greater vision through the ecstatic that mixes opposites – Rilke saying, "For Beauty's nothing/ but beginning of Terror we're still just able to bear" (Rilke 1939, 21) Or we go beyond through the sheer fun of meeting another fully, immediately, all four feet in and the other's too; Or, or, or, the wonderful gifts of nature, of friendship, of art, all bestow the mirth of being alive, the pleasure.

But trauma happens and forces toward healing that stirs up this kind of rhythm of two steps forward, successfully assimilating and housing some of the trauma's damage, and twenty steps back into the core of its pain again. What I suggest here is the rhythm of healing the psychoid field confers, that disrupt the old markers of progress. Instead or also we are conducted into the whole of it: a coincidence of trauma and healing that yield the possibility to be, to thrive.

We learn some of our personal myth and see some of our patient's personal myth, and see some of the whole mythmaking of meaning that includes our personal response. Those of us particularly caught by religion, as was Jung, also pursue who is the author of all these multiple meanings. We are thus ushered into conversation with God (or what we name otherwise).

The First Witness

For such arduous sustained work we depend on an other as the first witness that something happened to us who wants to know what happened to us. This other listens intently as we try to speak of what is unspeakable. Recognition of what took place and what effects go on occurring now – like weeping, pacing, staring without words – defeats denial. We need that first witness who also looks with us to the forces in us and between us that seek liberation from this entrapment (Ulanov 2009/2014, 198-200, 205-210).

The analyst for her part, if she is that other, must retain deep contact with her own inaugural image, her own root, her own thinking and feeling, not fleeing upwards into intellectualizations of what is happening in psychoid field nor in reactive defense against its dismantling of usual orienting markers. Living in the larger bowl, so to speak, the analyst arrives there from her own experience of destructiveness/creativeness as a fellow citizen with her patient, a sister refugee from ordered predictable world of personality number 1 as Jung names it in *Memories Dreams, Reflections*, and from the collective 'spirit of the times' as he names it in his *Red Book*. The analyst listens for the news conveyed in symptoms, bizarre images and swirls of associations, accepting as Jung's soul pronounces in *The Red Book* that the mystery of life is that it has no laws (Jung 2009, 298).

Experience precedes knowing. As an equal with her analysand feeling the jumble in the psychoid layer, sensing breathing rhythms, body movements, intuiting seeds of potential meaning in the attack on meaning, they look for that bridge between the patient's dissociated states, to hear the "story not told, and which as a rule no one knows of ... the patient's secret, the rock against which he is shattered" (Jaffé 1963, 117; also cited in McAllister 2014, 159). The priceless individuality of each person demands a unique response: "the solution to the problem is always an individual one" (ibid., 131).

The Second Witness

We also depend on the second witness of the psyche itself (Ulanov 2009/2014, 200, 210-212). What images is it offering to deal with what is happening to us, to our analysand: "The unconscious mentality is an instinctive one ... it does not 'think'.... It simply creates an image that answers to the conscious situation. This image contains as much thought as feeling and is anything rather than a product of rationalistic reflection" (Jung 1953, para 289; also cited in Sullivan 2010, 7). Psyche is always pushing at us through symptoms to get that shard of glass from trauma out of our system. Churning up new images in dreams, intruding fantasies, active imaginings to engage with what such images might express. The psyche itself badgers us with anxiety or harasses us with depression to jerk us awake, scare us into action. Our psyche gives us pictures in dreams, in repeating behaviors that portray what is going on, if we can understand it. For example, a young eighty-year-old woman reduced to shuffling along in sneakers for the last ten years due to unsatisfactory knee replacements, brings a first dream of going out but having to go back because she forgot her golden high heel shoes! What can the dream intend in picturing what is impossible to wear concretely, but calls up archetypal Cinderella-like shoes, glamorous psychic footwear necessary before she can go further, even in this late decade in her life.

Touching psychoid level of unconscious in synchronistic experiences awakens us to a bigger dimension in which we are now living, a beyond already here that is near, and hits us with terrific impact of meaning. The release is not back to ego categories and predictable 'spirit of the times,' but to the truth in the event that opens our hearts, makes us see the mess we got into from a different perspective. Maybe not ego defeat now but a sign on the road that shows the next direction into this bigger world where everything is. How to house that? Not now how to get back to adapt to collective expectations, but how to be re-minded (made mindful again), re-membered (aware again we are members) into this new possibility of finding our place in relation to the whatness *(quiddity)* to which we belong (see M. Stein 2014). We see beyond our teller's window to the entire bank we work for, respond with soul's all-out willingness to serve that greater firm, and through it to honor its origin from the beyond which it conveys. New possibilities in such meaningful occurrences elicit new options, and the verve to take them.

The trustworthiness of the first witness who listens intently to us moves us to risk following a hunch that comes up between us and that other, to try a different response than blaming the other for our distress. In the psychoid field analysand and analyst perform those prospective roles and live a more equal relationship, of two together facing elemental human experience that shows through the analysand's material. In example 1 (murder) I gave of psychoid event, my patient saw me both as analyst trained to do the job of analyzing and as a similar human finding her way with destructive and creative forces. Together we confront those forces in each other, in ourselves, between us, and engaging both of us together. We face a similar task how to house such forces, use them, apologize for failures and mistakes and feel pleased, even thrilled, when our efforts work. Options of response widen – to laugh, or finally to utter a word breaking our long silence, to try on aligning with and using these destructive and creative forces.

In addition, the way of proceeding is not linear in a psychoid field. A nudge, a scrap of memory, a child's immediacy of response – to wonder, to be open – joins our adult reflecting on a new possibility. Psychic energy begins slowly to move, or to stabilize from extremes into a steadier thrum. In example 1 I mentioned our confusion reigned. My patient said the look on my face showing I was in it too, made her know I was trustworthy, the work we were doing was trustworthy; she was trustworthy; we could count on it and each other.

Meaning Matters

Meaning matters. Recovering meaning makes living possible. But meaning often comes through the back door, not with flowers and a scroll declaring it elegantly, but, in the examples I gave, with tears, silence, utter self-doubt. Its method of coming is also different from reasoning, logic, direct progression by steps. Meaning hints, pulses in our body, something 'clicks.' Chance associations throw opposites together and reveal a larger unity between them without reducing either to the other nor fusing or mixing them. Each opposing content remains diverse as my patient and I remained so in the midst of psychoid currents. Odd hunches gradually widen tiny spaces between self and the dominating complex. Who would have thought goodness appears in confusion, deficit, doubt! Who would have thought hunches could accumulate wisdom! That something more cannot be lassoed into conscious understanding!

We know in a different way from usual reasoning. Sensing, feeling, intuiting, registering in body, in willingness of soul to respond, we answer with a whole heart to a whole world. This new experience changes our living. We respond with child's openness and adult's reflection to the impact of meaning. Jung sees such objective meaning as giving us absolute knowledge; we just know something but do not know how we know it; such meaning exists transcendently beyond consciousness and its categories and methods of understanding. (Jung 1952/1960, paras 931, 948; Jaffé 1963, 51).

Yet if we do not subjectively register the impact of this meaningful coincidence, it does not inscribe itself on us or our sense of something more, however we may define that. Our own sense of subjective I-ness is necessary to perceive what is objectively there. Our subjective response makes the objective fact of meaning accessible to us, and through us come into our culture, our family. Our subjective agency, our soul willingness to respond, is the path to objective meaning. In such experience we both find meaning that shows itself and make meaning visible in our response to it. This contributes to healing, as I said above, of mending personal trauma, and mending the splits in culture that deny meaning that binds us into a people (see also above, page 27).

The blanking of our mind in trauma that strips us of meaning occurs in totalitarian cultures where meaning is divested by the ruling body, be it a persecutory government, or authorities in our training group, or the head of the school, the chief of police. Either they are coercive or we project into them such bullying tactics. Totalitarian governments cover up such stripping, ransacking meaning by propaganda, putting a cover of lies over expunged truth. This makes citizens crazy (see Godsil 2014, 69-70). Meaning is looted from speech and action: thoughts may not be thought, words may not be said, questions not asked; even dreams must be hidden.

The astonishing implication is that our personal, subjective, even idiosyncratic responses to the larger dimension world that the psychoid level suggests and the synchronistic event discloses have to occur for the objective, self-subsistent meaning to become real to us and thus enter our human culture. Objective meaning thus lies within, that is, depends on our subjectivity; and, our subjectivity to feel really meaningful lies within, depends on objective independent meaning.

Why are these implications important? Because they directly address our experience of meaning in life, that meaning exists and affects our healing where we find where we belong and how to serve the whole. For example, Jung's notion of individuation I understand not that you or I achieve wholeness (see above, page 21). I do not know any fully individuated people. And analysts are certainly not examples, witness our food fights when we hurl back and forth psychological terms in combat with each other. Individuation means, I suggest, finding our place or path in the whole scheme. So we can say, and feel lucky to do so, as my late good friend did upon his retirement from a long teaching career, "Looking back, I see I was where I belonged." He had found his path; that meaning sustained him through painful losses, affliction of illness. Jung says finding such meaningfulness to our own lives is what heals. What we do matters, indeed, has significance for life itself. I feel grateful for what you discover and put into the psychological atmosphere, the spiritual reality in which we all dwell whether we know it or not.

Of course our process of meaning-making as in symbol-formation helps shape how objective meaning shows itself. The degree to which we gather personal associations of family, lovers, friends, mentors, flesh out our symbols. As do associations that spring from locations in neighborhoods – whether the smell of asphalt pavement on hot summer streets, or cooling breezes wafting through a leafy glen, let alone the specific archetypal images that penetrate what meaning appears. In the moment of receiving the event's impact and making more of it in our response of fear and awe, we add to its meaningfulness.

We need those first witnesses, whether analyst, spouse, author, and we need the second witness of images, sounds, even smells, or textures that the psyche may offer. We want to know the "true God from the true God," not a God we cobble together, nor a God so distant from our meaning-making there is no contact, no recognition. Jung was looking for what we are seeking – the interpenetration or bridge between everyday reality (of personality 1) and the ages (of personality 2), that together make up one entire world of earth and all its inhabitants, and cosmos, through history, humanity and the heavens beyond. Jung suffered a division (but not a split, he said), between his two worlds; he sees their "play and counterplay ... played out in every individual" (Jaffé 1963, 45, 47, 48; see also Saban 2014, 17). Of himself, Jung says, "The difference between most people and myself is that for me the "dividing walls" are transparent.... I perceive the processes going on in the background and this gives me an inner certainty ... perceiving the stream of life" (ibid, 355-356).

Jung coined words to describe this distinction – ego and self, spirit of times and spirit of depths; I would add, the Self and the reality it mediates beyond Self. For me Self is not God but that in us that knows about God. Our subjective response is integral to meaning coming into view, and when it does, as something outside us addressing us and inside us knowing about this something more outside us, we register *its* existence, not just our participation in it.

Healing

How does experience of the psychoid level and the fact that meaning matters effect our clinical intent to aid healing? What does healing look like? It appears as a greater capacity to think new thoughts, feel new feelings, admit various intuitions, engage imaginatively with more possibilities that heretofore never came on the scene or if they started to were dismissed by us. That is what healing looks like. Winnicott calls it more elbow-room. Bion calls it developing alpha function to translate bombarding beta elements into actual thoughts and feelings, arriving at emotional truth of the moment. On a more personal level I have heard analysands say, it is a wish to love; I feel wonder: I feel increasing space between the tyranny of complex with its preemptive interpretations and the fact of my self.

Clinical experience has shown me the condition of being depressed may slowly transform into a symptom (Ulanov 2007,

21-23). Depression still strikes but the patient notices it and traces down the trigger that set such suffering in motion; consciousness intercedes. Depression is no longer a condition that describes the total living space, but is an interrupter. The person has additional possibilities, feels plugged into sources of reasoning related to living energy that can be found. One feels not just the soothing but the rectifying of dreaming, or, if not at night when asleep, more aware of the currents of a dreaming state there also when awake. Imagination embroiders immediate experience, enriching its quality by funny or touching associations or even associations of grieving that show the larger picture, rescuing us from gloom and from cheeriness, for the real thing, the sentiment Iris Murdoch expresses: Goodness – it is good for nothing; it is. (Murdoch 1969, 254). We are moved to gratitude for the generosity of reality.

5. Dread of Transition, and an Additional Matrix

Experience of the psychoid quality of the unconscious brings an addition to the notion of psychological transition. Winnicott describes a space an infant moves into on the basis of experiences of union with the mothering one. The infant makes a transition from absolute to relative dependence on the mother and begins finding and creating self and world through loved objects – bear, doll, edge of blanket – that form an infant's first symbol. In relation to these transitional objects the infant moves between "fantasy and fact ... inner object and external object ... from (magical) omnipotent control to control by manipulation (involving muscle erotism and coordination pleasure) ... between *primary creativity and objective perception based on reality testing*" (Winnicott 1971, 6, 9, 11). Such transition is joyous on the whole. Play shows gradual mastery of forces of creating and destroying – building up a tower of blocks and knocking it down! Rituals develop – at bedtime putting the bear only on the right side and putting one's tiny finger in the 'bloop' on its back (a loop of cloth that served the manufacturer to mount the toy for display) to secure bear fur close to the body. (see Ulanov 1996/2004, 392-396, 413-418; see also Ulanov 2001a, 14-16, 30-31, 39-40, 95-96).

Another Transition

Contra the joy and fun associated with Winnicott's ideas of transition (transitional object, transitional space, transition by the infant), transition into the psychoid quality of the unconscious can induce dread. We may abhor the psychoid as undoing of inner structures we rely upon, fraying boundaries we need for definition of self and world, mixing up time senses, space senses, and other senses we have carefully differentiated to discover self sense. Instead, touching the psychoid can make us feel we enter not a unified reality but boundlessness itself.

In addition, the psychoid dimension moves us out of cultural assumptions, motifs we have relied upon. They are not so much invalidated, for we may and usually do return to familiar cultural customs, but now we are conscious of their limits; they are relative, no longer taken for granted as dependable truths and the way things are done. We succumb to dread of cultural disintegration. On the positive side, we may feel on the edge of a whole new way of perceiving reality, for example, experiencing events or emotions, ideas, insights, not as sequential but simultaneous. The new is here but so still is the old. A man said, for example, yes, his mother's depression still takes up all the oxygen in the room but also present, he sees, is her courage in enduring and not being vanquished by this experience of deepest doldrums that had killed her sister. Both exist now together. What seemed either/or yields to diversity of options, of absence of certainties, of amplitude of possibilities and a perception that pattern and contingency coexist.

On the negative side, our transition toward greater awareness of the psychoid quality of the unconscious may coincide with collective shifts from old interpretations to new ones of cultural myths underlying our civilization. Literal meanings give way to symbolic ones. Perennial myths undergo reinterpretations to new forms, but we can be living in the transitional time and feel loss of truth we took for granted (see Baring and Cashford 1993, 608, 666).

No wonder Jung reflecting on *The Red Book* venture said he needed to repeat aloud the realities of his everyday life–I am a psychiatrist, I live at ... am married to ... have 5 children. Such 'reality testing' gives points of anchor in the shifting currents of dream next to fantasy, body hunches as powerful as thought. Repeated ignorance of what was going on left Jung feeling nauseated (Jaffé 1963, 188-189; Jung 2009, 235). The markers defining living space fade and what Bion calls 'nameless dread' supervenes (Bion 1962, 96 and 1984, 77).

This state of meaninglessness where we cannot process into word, image, or narrative what is happening is alarming, horrible. Heaps of fragments, fractions of whole objects drift around; intense affects switch to their opposites, hence confuse and assault and we feel helpless to incarnate our lives. Transition does not proceed apace to self and world but tips us into absurdity, what Jung called "nonsensical"; nothing makes coherent sense, no line of development can be sketched. Chaos looms (Jung 2009, 235; Jaffé 1963, 177).

Even more frightening, what we relied on to guide us - our principles, our ethical standard, our confidence in our own perception, our spiritual maxim connected to truth, what Jung called in *The Red Book* our ruling principle, is here completely useless. It does not work anymore (see example Ulanov 2013, 59-63). This chief axiom is what we call the good, the true and differentiate from what we designate as bad, evil. It is our rudder through the currents of life, even our lifeline when in times of greatest stress and breakdown. But here this governing beacon itself breaks down. We employ it and it has no effect, usually because other and previously neglected affects, impulses, thoughts charge forward to dominate us. This renders us feeling dangerously helpless, cast adrift, unable to get a handle on what is happening.

Jung sees we must sacrifice this sovereign principal because it is too one-sided and oppresses opposite perceptions and tendencies in ourselves that now must be developed. But the moment of discovering that this guide is impotent is to see the ground beneath our feet is no longer solid enough to stand on; we plunge into nowhere. It is here, I believe, we fear going out of our minds, as Jung did, thinking he was headed into a psychosis. (Jaffé 1963, 176, 188).

Matrix as Container

A usual interpretation of this state of affairs traces its cause to lack of maternal container at the beginning of life, offering a diagnosis of attachment disorder. Its healing may come through provision of maternal reverie on the part of the analyst in the face of the analysand's silent dread rendering her or him unreachable, or noisy dread attacking the analyst's and their own ability to think, to link up communications. Reverie means the analysand's riotous and terrifying affects and splintered thoughts get projected into the analyst as maternal container, who processes them into detoxified thinkable thoughts and feelings and gives them back to the patient. Slowly the analysand grows capable of processing his or her own experience, in Bion's terms gains their own alpha function to translate bombarding beta elements into liveable experiences. (MacCalister 2014, 165-167).

I am not questioning the value of such a container. But what of those of us who never had it? Is that the only recourse for healing? Jung lacked it, not finding it in his own mother. That privation again burst onto the scene in his adult life when suffering traumatic separation from Freud and from the world of psychoanalysis in which Jung was a successful leader. Jung looked to nature itself and later to diverse cultures, mythologies, religions, alchemies, fairy tales and mythopoetic imaginings as alternate matrices and dialogue partners for anchoring his own life. "[He] created a matrix for himself using the written heritage he studied ... to heal himself and to create an entire psychology based on explorations into his self" (Cavalli 2014, 194; see also Wirtz 2014, 243-247). Note, too, his father initially made these traditions available to Jung by giving him at an early age free run of his library and teaching him Latin. Jung found another matrix than the containing one. Indeed, I remember laughing out loud reading in *The Red Book* when Jung is complaining of the "hard struggle" to reach his soul, the soul snaps at him: "I am not your mother" (Jung 2009, 236). The soul does not function as a container!

An Additional Matrix

Another matrix in addition to the mothering receptacle, and a different function from containing need to be recognized, especially in facing psychoid experiences. I suggest a matrix – whether cultural, of nature or of something else – that we experience as *interpenetrating* more than containing. An analysand, for example, found such a matrix in the actual building of her childhood home. It was not so much that she felt held in the building's architecture, but that she felt penetrated by diverse aspects – the rough stucco of the walls, the sheen of brocade on the curtains, the scent of the sheets, the ruby and sapphire colors in the rugs. Her experience reminded me of the art critic Adrian Stokes' emphasis on unconstraint in his comment, "A house is a womb substitute in whose passages we move with freedom" (Stokes 1972, 78). Dependence upon, and dialogue with such a matrix conjugate through mutual piercing, permeation, influence, acting upon, inclining toward.

Benefits and Limits of the Container Image, and of the Interpenetrating Matrix

The 'container' image, currently prominent in discussion among analysts and in relation to attachment theory and aspects of brain research operates within the mother archetype. Primary emphasis focuses on what benefits of maternal reverie accrue (or fail to) to the baby, without equivalent emphasis on how the subjectivity of the mothering one gets wooed into being, in addition to and in distinction from being a mothering figure. This is also generally the case in reference to the analyst and analysand though there is much literature on countertransference, but little on the permeating influence of the patient on the subjectivity of the analyst, her life, her sense of self apart from her work.

In my life as a mother and in listening intently to my analysands tell of their being mothers, there is a life-changing effect exerted on the mothering one, wooing one into that state of endless translating an infant's or a patient's affect and sensation into feelable, thinkable bits that go to make up the self incarnating in the space-time world. But equally strong is what happens to/in the subjectivity of this 'containing' one. If that is neglected, then the individuality, the subjectness of the mothering one can be eclipsed in the vitality of mothering. Motherhood offers teaching to be a self in addition to teaching to be a mother and forces differentiation from one's maternal capacities. I remember in my son's teenage years my all but yelling around the house when overly taxed, I am a person too, not just a selfobject! (see also, as applied to analysis, Sullivan 2010, 4). Neglect of those tutorings in one's subjectivity can result in the mothering one's personality becoming engulfed by the mothering/containing mode, to the detriment of becoming all of oneself, for and as oneself.

Enid Balint wrote a wonderful piece about the subjectivity of the mother in her parental role: "This feed-back process between mother and baby presupposes an interaction between two active partners which, I think, differentiates it from projection and introjection in which one of them is only a passive object" (Balint 1993, 51).

The contrast I see here between the containing and interpenetrating matrices shows several parts. As Balint says, containing turns round the infant or analysand projecting into the mothering one or analyst what is indigestible in the self and then reintrojecting it detoxified by the mother or analyst, back into the self in more assimilated form. The two mix, merge and mingle together, eventually to differentiate into distinct subjectivities. The initial hierarchical power dynamic softens into a more equal relationship but not a fully mutual one.

In the interpenetrating mode, different from the containing mode, the matrix, be it human or nonhuman, is in a mutual influencing, imbuing relation with the infant/analysand, each acting upon the other's subjectivity while remaining distinct, not merged, but other. Each influences the other with a potency to effect the other, shaping and being shaped by the other, as a "play and counterplay," much like what Jung describes goes on between the worlds of personality 1 and 2 (Jaffé 1963, 45). Those two centers of personality do not contain each other, neither everyday life of personality 1 enclosing personality 2 of the timeless ages, nor the converse. Each has its own center and they penetrate each other, have power to affect each other, but do not merge or mix. One may erupt into the other, but they remain distinct, like conversational partners in deep discussion (Jung 1950a/1959, para 235; see also, Saban 2013, 14-15).

The container image in analysis, applying to the analyst, too often gets one-sided emphasis, perpetuating inequality in the relationship, the dominant translator to the less equal translated one, the container over the contained one and neglect of the converse. Jung's essay on marriage emphasizes this one-way container image. One partner is the container for the other who is the contained one. The roles are not interchangeable. The essay leaves off with this sort of split with which Jung himself struggled (Jung 1931/1954, paras 331-334).

In analysis, although there is much literature on the analyst's countertransference, there is more to be done by focusing on how the analyst's subjectivity is shaped by the analysand. This focus concerns the relation of such work to the analyst's life, not the analyst's work on the 'case.' What I am emphasizing is the patient's power to penetrate, contribute to the analyst's subjectness. An example is a patient asking me a decisive question, not about him or my relation to him, nor about our shared work in the analysis, but about my relation to something in my life evident in the session. The question pierced my subjectivity. I realized I had never asked such a question, nor had it ever come up in any analysis I had engaged. That question changed my life; from it, twelve years later, came a book.[8] Sharing experience of the psychoid level of unconscious, I suggest, does just that kind of penetrating.

An additional source of matrix with which interpenetrating happens shows a more equal, mutual relation between analyst and analysand – both parties are affected and change and grow, get blocked, stuck, overloaded, overwhelmed. The path toward fuller living, toward healing, emphasizes the intimate involvement of each shaped by the other, not identical but mutually affected and contributed to by the other. Recognition of this kind of matrix makes for more spaciousness in each and in their relationship.

The Unconscious Psyche, and the Soul, as Additional Matrices

In addition, in relation to the second witness of what the psyche itself offers in image, impulse, nub of imagination, fastening to fugitive thought a bit gleaming in a dream, there is the matrix of the unconscious. Jung says, speaking of the artist, but I believe it applies to anyone attuned to our 'interior' life, "the creative work arises from the unconscious depths ... from the realm of the Mothers" (Jung 1950/1966, para 159). Those mothers are not containers translating our inchoate thoughts and affects into nontoxic feelable and thinkable contents. In fact, we work hard to translate 'their' thoughts. We work hard with the images of these Mothers to sort out our idiosyncratic way of understanding them based on our personal biographies, cultural contexts, and to discern which

8. See Ulanov 2001b. My patient asked me in our session, having not needed to heed my warning to patients that I was afflicted with poison ivy and to cancel the session if they feared contagion. "Had I ever analysed why I kept getting poison ivy?" he asked. I was subject to annual outbreaks, but this one was particularly extreme. With shock, I realized I had never asked that question nor had anyone else. It inaugurated a long inquiry. After several years of such searching, it was as if poison ivy, a notorious contact allergy, had been dragged into the psychic sphere as I began to dream of it. With that, after five decades of yearly combat, *I ceased to get poison ivy attacks.* I do not reduce this physical allergy to psychic causes, but I do see that the psyche can make use of physical ailments to carry what one is still unable to carry psychologically.

archetypal images arise in us for this "something profoundly alive in the soul" (ibid). (This may turn out to be a differentiation of the feminine, much needed in our culture in the West.)

Of great importance is the soul's announcement in *The Red Book* that neither its nature nor its relationship to Jung is motherly. Maternal containment is not the function of this soul! This soul wants relationship, sacrifice, atonement. Note that the soul for Jung, as for much of religion, is gendered as feminine. 'She' wants Jung to get with it, see his pretensions and bombast, to get in right relation with the whole of life, find his proportionate place, not dominate others as their shepherd or prophet. He is to live his ownmost life which includes even vigorous arguments with his soul in which his soul also radically changes. Remember Jung getting 'her' to relinquish back to earth human warm-blooded loving, not to abscond with it to heaven or offer mortals the bribe of serve me the soul and my salvation now and we mortals will get salvation in some immortal afterlife. No! says Jung. Our loving is ours and we work for our life here, and so should you work for the good of humanity, Jung insists, not for your salvation in some heaven. And the soul yields! This lively contretemps differs greatly from the containment model (Jung 2009, 344-345).

This interpenetrating role of soul recalls earlier discussion in chapter 1 of its function as intermediate 'receiver and transmitter' between ego and unconscious, reflecting up and down from each to each salient images to be united in a whole life, worked for in the process of individuation. It reflects unconscious images 'up' to the ego, and ego images 'down' to the unconscious, so each point of view comes into contact with the other. They meet and interpenetrate. Their interpenetration may instigate the transcendent function that creates a resulting new image or attitude that symbolizes the suffering of the previous conflict lifted to a new level that feels like reconciliation, peace. The ego, that is, our sense of I-ness, has the conviction that this new symbol is not one we did or could invent; it feels like a blessing from something more beyond our human efforts. This process of conflict, meeting, symbol, insight goes on throughout life, up to its end. There is no final containment that concludes it, but ongoing interpenetrating instead.

In such an intermediary role, we might speculate that soul itself instances coincidence of opposites, the unconscious and the ego and all the opposites they symbolize. The soul acknowledges opposites without their diminishment or fusion, each retaining its own territory but surpassed in their dwelling together and yielding to new forms in the process of individuation.

Back to Murder

In the example of my analysand's murderous mother, I heard from my patient that her mother had said she was liberating her babies to a better heaven. I imagined this mother was seemingly without awareness of the shadow intent of seeking her own emancipation from the burdens of motherhood by dispatching her offspring. So great was the pressing for freedom that it was located in heaven, not possible on earth. Nor was it seen that such freedom meant killing off obstacles in the here and now, even one's children. I imagined she could not face more offspring after an interval of some years between the first four children and now these next three who were the intended objects of her attack. Even when there were just the first four, an older sibling overheard her mother suggest to their father that she and her husband leave the children and go away together. Hearing that from my patient, I thought the mother already felt overwhelmed, if not crushed. For, indeed, she wanted to bring upstairs where her daughter, my patient, and her brother were sleeping, an infant boy, I imagined, to include in the dispatch from this life. But her husband intervened, saying, keep the baby downstairs. I imagined the mother was beyond mothering, exhausted by its endless duties to seven children and wanted some life of her own self, which only seemed to appear in trying to get snatches of reading. My patient said her mother was often carrying around a book.

Although returned to a functioning state after arrest, hospitalization and shock treatments, this mother endured threatening anger from her husband if she missed any doses of her medicine, him yelling, you will be locked up in a hellhole of an institution (the condition of mental hospitals then in that part of the country). They lived within the working class economically hence no thought of hiring outside help, and within a religious framework in which protection against conceiving more babies was forbidden. I imagined the father felt fear every day returning from work whether he would find liveable functioning or threat of life-killing emotions.

How could this mother accommodate her personal soul life, relate to Mothers of the deep who care about life's force, creating a sense of self and beyond? I imagined that question in this mother's life was reduced to laundry, cooking, cleaning, dishes, all the tasks of managing alone a brood of children. Her vision of freedom to be and become located in distant heaven, cloaked killing to get there, and got locked up, medicated, guarded against, I believe, for the rest of her life.

My patient, however, suffered the residue of 'there is something wrong with me' that extended all the way back to her small girl self. Not only because of this dreadful event but because no one ever talked about it in the family, except in threats to be locked up if something like that surfaced again. In fact, my patient spontaneously lied about it, so imbued was she by the family declaring this event was off limits. She described that months later in the basement of their house, after her mother had finally returned from the hospital and shock treatments, her mother asking her and her brother what was this bill from the hospital for stitches? My patient remembered she immediately lied, saying the stitches were because they cut themselves on a glass bottle that their mother told them not to play with. As a small girl my patient took the blame on herself, saying that this was not to protect her mother, but from terror her mother might erupt in violence again, and she must not arouse her.

No talking about this event occurred, let alone letting the children speak of their terror of feeling killable. My analysand was told she was never to tell what happened. In addition, she felt horror that she hated her mother out of fear of some break-out of brutal force. She related mostly to her mother in unexpressed anger that kept the mother under watch but brought no solace or mutual recognition of the great hurt they both experienced in this trauma. Nor did they mourn all they had lost of a close, happy, mother-daughter loving. However, my analysand took offence when an authoritative person in her life dismissed her mother with the comment, "Well, she was psychotic." With tears in her eyes, my patient said in outrage, "as if that was all my mother was, that she wasn't a person!" There were the seeds of compassion.

The Psychoid and the Matrix

As I said earlier (page 55ff), when touching the psychoid quality of the unconscious, the container(s) that have worked for us and the guidelines called by Jung our ruling principles, no longer do so. Trauma does that too and we are left not just bereft but splintered, as if the ground under our feet is cracking up. What to rely on? We are falling into Nowhere, or, as one patient put it, as if outside the spaceship and the connecting line to it is fraying, and then what? Spinning into spaceless void!

The matrix of the Mothers of the deep know about the void and expect us, so to speak, to come to know about it too, as well as keeping in touch with the wellspring of life, what Jung calls the "self-replenishing abundance of living creatures, a wealth beyond our fathoming" (Jung 1946/1954, para 366), "the fountainhead" (Jung 1956/1974, para 449). The psychoid can be either and both – the loss of all ego grounding and perspective in the boundless, the plenty, the abundance. I think of the philosopher Dorothy Emmet's words in relation to the terrifying and wondrous otherness of what transcends our ego perspective, or, indeed, the perspective of our whole psyche, and the inevitable ambivalence of presenting "the analogue of the transcendent in the forms of the phenomenal, of the infinite and the finite" (Emmet 1957, 105).

Two different realms of being interpenetrate, each precious and mysterious. Their meeting recalls Bright's recommendation of the analytic attitude of ambiguity when working with his patient: not-knowing and crediting what the analysand's material hints at, shown in the willingness (what I call the soul's capacity) "for two people to engage, in awe and excitement ... with forces beyond their comprehension, in the service of the individuation of both" (Bright 2014, 103).

Our need for a matrix, whatever its form, is for a boundary making a space in which to receive and explore whole chunks of unprocessed experience so their livingness can come into conscious existing in the world with others. What has not been contained and processed into thinkable and feelable bits remains dissociated and presses for recognition through somatic symptoms, compulsive behaviors, emotional obsessions, free-floating complexes of anxiety, dread, depression. They are acted out by us but bypass consciousness, not yet connecting present losses with early ones unremembered but suffered, what Winnicott calls our earliest psychotic anxieties, our "*breakdown that has already been experienced*" (Winnicott 1989, 90), what Cavalli calls a '"constant threat to stability", a "no-man's land ... of unrealized trauma" (Cavalli 2014, 195). Self and ego play a part in this reaching for emotional truth of our own experience. In their mutual penetration we live in a bigger world (Sullivan 2010, 54-5). Life presses us to admit this enlarged vision, as if under orders of some sovereign authority.

Such is not the 'metaphysical police' Jung complains of in Joyce's *Ulysses*, of sentimentality on top of brutality (Jung 1949/1966 paras 182-184), nor restoration of the persona (Jung 1953/1966, para 259) of return to cracked shells of religious belief. Rather, this sense of authority is, I believe, the something more that Jung is seeking and acknowledging at the same time he is saying he does not know. After all, he approaches his numinous experiences not only with his reductive analytic method (though some critics say not enough of this), but also his synthetic prospective method. Where was this heading, not only in terms of personal integration of new bits of livingness, but toward what or whom, into relationship with what? Jung often uses the word God and protests why not, it has always been used and everyone knows what it means (see Dyer 2000). At the same time, Jung may disavow religious reference to God, saying it is the God-image he speaks of, as if we could completely separate the image of God from the reality to which it points. (Jung 1976, 522-223, 269).

The Uncontainable

One more important point about an additional matrix as interpenetrating needs to be noted. The Hintons (father and three sons) have criticized Jung's notion of *unus mundus* as Jung's ideal, his searching for foundational, all–encompassing container "where 'opposites' are transcended by unity" (L. Hinton III, 2011, 376). This unified world is the goal, the telos of life's energy. What is not adequately seen, they suggest, is that such a vision "has often had unpredictable and sometimes disastrous ethical consequences" (ibid, 377). As an example, L. Hinton IV gives the exclusion of someone suffering from Alzheimer's from such a goal of unity, because not seen as a subject but as a disease category, both on a personal level and not as part of a one world with others. Drawing on the thought of Levinas, a result of a whole world goal can be the "'objectification' of the subjectivity of the person ... transforming them into an 'Alzheimer-ed subject' and impeding empathic connection" (L. Hinson IV, 2011, 381). D. Hinton presents our agoraphobic panic-like reaction to the speed of modernity in urban spaces whose redesign lacks a central containing function. Munch's painting of "The Scream" illustrates the absence of security of a one-world containment in "a nitemare of fear and vertigo, the modern cityscape as a draining place of chaos, anomie, and excessive hurry" (D. Hinton 2011, 386). A. Hinton presents his research on genocides as a result of the repudiation of any truths that conflict with the foundational unified truth we may espouse that contains all opposites and implies ultimacy as *the* truth. Getting rid of opposing points of view and of those who hold them generates the possibility of genocides: "But the pure Truth does not exist in the sense of a universal objective reality. What we have instead are a multitude of truths linked to different instantiations of being.... This tension and dread suggest a dialectic of genocide "(A. Hinton 2011, 393).

Apropos the Hintons' criticism of Jung advancing a foundational truth, Jung does say science was his way to "extricate myself from that chaos" (Jaffé 1963, 188) of the primordial images recounted in *The Red Book*, an attempt that may seem to fasten on fixed progression of stages of individuation (analysing persona, ego, shadow, anima/animus, self complexes) and on one type of authoritative image (mandala) so everyone can arrive at the same unitary world. Yet contra that possible impression, in his *Red Book* Jung exhorts us not to imitate his way but to find our own mystery play, our particular experiences of descent into the unconscious and its collective forceful themes. Jung also repeatedly asserts that all theories are subjective confessions and describes in his autobiography how what he offered through his works were in fact "stations along my life's way ... tasks imposed from within; their source was a fateful compulsion ... things that assailed me from within myself" (Jaffé 1963, 222; see also Saban 2014, 22).

I would suggest that Jung himself proposes throughout and at the end of his life that there are no final, defining (containing) conclusions. *The Red Book* ends with Jung saying he must go back to the Middle Ages to deal with the barbarian in himself, that is, the process of what he later will call individuation is not finished but ongoing. He turns to diversity in studying the myths, alchemies and religions of many cultures to find the rivers that run through them, not to build a once and for all edifice. Taking up *The Red Book* project again decades later in 1959, he abandons it immediately and in mid-sentence, turning instead to what presses him inwardly, so that in the last two decades of his life he writes over nine major works, let alone a huge correspondence and autobiography (Jaffé 1971, 99-100). In his autobiography he eschews a final truth, saying, "I can only ... 'tell stories.' Whether or not the stories are 'true' is not the problem. The only question is whether what I tell is *my* truth" (Jaffé 1963, 3). At the end of that volume he says, "I am astonished, disappointed, pleased with myself. I am distressed, depressed, rapturous. I am all these things at once, and cannot add up the sum ... There is nothing I am quite sure about. I have no definite convictions – not about anything really." This is a soul, a man in process still: "life is – or has – meaning and meaninglessness" (Jung 2009, 358, 359). And I remember the startling sentences in *The Red Book*, "Life itself has no rules. That is its mystery and its unknown law" (Jung 2009, 298).

Nonetheless, I agree with all the Hintons emphasizing what is excluded by truths that we seize upon as *the* truth, with no awareness of all that is left out. That repeats what Jung discovered about our valuable 'ruling principle' that omits our 'incapacities' that need development, both in our personal life and in our collective life together. This emphasis strengthens my sense that more than one kind of matrix is needed, containers, yes, but not finally nor always the best. An interpenetrating matrix seems true to life to me, how we subtly influence each other in many particular ways, in local contexts, and even across nations through news and through cultures. It is through that particularity we experience the nexus to the All, the whole, which we never reach nor comprehend. It is not a product, not a commodity called truth. It is an image of desiring and growing toward the uncontainable.

A Leap Perhaps?

Rather than a foundational one unitary world, I sense opening to a different way of perceiving reality. It fills with many objects, varied options, diversity of perceptions, multiplicity of meanings, a reality that environs us like air with its many currents, or earth with its different textures of soil and rock, like the vagaries and flamings of fire, the waves of deep water that sustain all life. Perhaps we are just now on the cusp of a leap to a different vision, not in degree, but in kind, of a linked up amplitude that shows a oneness that bespeaks all our differences like the Lord's endorsement of plurality of languages in the felling of the ideal of only one true language in the Tower of Babel attempt. This plurality does not mean chaos but plenitude, many and one, like the Pentecost flame of spirit that everyone understood in her and his own language, so different from ordinary known conceptions of what is possible that those overhearing those gathered into this spirit blowing where it wills, thought them drunk. Here the opposites show a secret, (or open!) handshake; what Sedgwick calls "a deep intimacy of chaos with order"(Sedgwick 2011, 84), like indeterminacy built into certainty, essence as epiphanies. Such an interpenetration of levels with each other reminds me of Jung's description of deep unconscious as fountainhead, such a profusion, a blooming.

In the background of the Hintons' criticism of Jung and of Jung's emphasis on the process of experiencing rather than a fastening on the truth, is the question, I believe, that is a major one for this twenty-first century. How to give heart soul mind and strength to what we perceive and what addresses us as truth while at the same time recognizing others do the same to different truths? Of course we identify with our truth and tend to identify it with ultimate truth. Yet we do know at the same time, this precious truth, like a revelation, is a mystery. In our limits, our finiteness, we see its veracity and are moved to enjoin it. But can we simultaneously not-know its final ultimacy? We feel it to be supreme, but can we see we cannot know its infinite dimensions? Is our task to carry both committing and not-knowing, so that though we love the truth we believe in with our whole heart, we do not turn it into a stick with which to beat our neighbor? This is the process – to give all-out and not-know for certain, not conclude, indeed leave it up to the subject of such truth to make its way, with us following. Hence the door stays open on our path though we are devoted to this path. That makes room for the different neighbor, a neighbor for whom we are different.

Something More

This matter and meaning of something more leads us to look into spiritual elements that turn up in, indeed fuel, clinical work. And what are they? Are they moments of meaning that we craft and respond to, from which we create symbols? Is there a meaningfulness there showing itself to us in that nexus of finite and infinite that Dorothy Emmet sees as the focus of religion, and that Jung says are the only things worth writing his autobiography about: "In the end the only events in my life worth telling are those when the imperishable world irrupted into this transitory one" (Jaffé 1963, 4).

These elements of spirit are there but a sort of collective avoidance of naming them exists, lest we lose our freedom to explore what is, because of feeling crowded to comply with what should be. Who or what presses us to open to the something more? What pushes us not to settle on named containers or settle for no name, but to look further into the dissociations that make us live at half-mast instead of full? This inquiring into gods and demons within and between us is also to ask where from, how come, to what do they lead us?

Soul questions, spirit questions emerge in addition to psychological exploration.[9] Who authors these notions? Jung notes our dependence not on a final conclusion identified as *the* truth, but on a process, an experiencing, that ushers us toward awareness of something more and its independent existence: "He man [sic] cannot conquer the tremendous polarity of his nature on his own resources; he can only do so through the terrifying experience of a

9. Again I would note that spirit, soul, and at times psyche as well are used interchangeably, and at times only one term is used to the neglect of the others (Main 2007, 24ff). I see psyche referring to our conscious and unconscious processes, spirit as referring to a collective dimension in which we all dwell even though we may experience personal impacts of spirit as a superhuman force moving through us, and soul as embodied in us as individuals that locates connection to God or to what we put in place of God as ground of our being. We could hazard that we are after something more and that these notions are used separately and together to symbolize that in different ways and emphases.

psychic process that is independent of him, that works *him* rather than he *it*" (Jung 1954/1958, para 446).

Jung emphasizes throughout his work the self-regulating nature of psyche that compensates ego excesses and lacks through dreams and symptoms. Jung hypothesizes the center of such regulating is Self, the point, the ordering archetype and the circumference of psyche conscious and unconscious (Jaffé 1963, 386): "The self is not only the centre but also the whole circumference which embraces conscious and unconscious; it is the centre of this totality, just as the ego is the centre of the conscious mind" (Jung 1953, para 44).

The relation of Self and ego is interpenetrating I am suggesting, not containing. Each of these two centers of consciousness within the human psyche, ego and Self, personality 1 and personality 2, effects its own mode of awareness and cannot contain the other (Jung 1950/1959, paras 117-235; see also Saban 2013, 17-20). Each has precious value. They may conflict, indeed grievously, but two such vantage points of awareness can aid us in times of strife too. What stymies our ego projects may in fact fulfill the Self, or we might reject the Self project in favor of the ego goal. Either way we are moved into experience of expanding to a greater spaciousness within and without, to see in our century Plato's two horses pulling the same chariot. Both belong to us; we need both; we fill out to greater range, to sense of something more and desire to make room for both.

Images of Something More, East and West

Jung found in his treatment of Christianity "the element of Indian healing" according to Collins and Molchanov, "specifically the continuing presence of the self-regulating atman from the Upanishads" that was the heart of transformation in the mandala and at the heart of the transcendent function, they contend (Collins and Molchanov 2013, 55).

To focus libido on the Self is to remove libido – as our energy of attention, of our attachment – from outer objects and from inner objects. Jung sees Christ, like the atman in Indian tradition, as a major symbol of the Self: "the Indian idea of the atman, whose personal and cosmic modes of being form an exact parallel to the psychological idea of the self" (Jung 1946/1954, para 474). In his treatment of the Christian mass, Jung takes up the "Round Dance" of Christ with his disciples, which in the apocryphal *Acts of John,* substitute for the Last Supper. Concentrating all libido on Christ and circling round him as the focal point effects an interpenetration of periphery and nucleus. Is this point analogous to what Leslie Stein, considering Jung and Tantra, refers to as the 'bindu,' the dot symbolizing "Siva's concentrated being" that Jung calls "the source of the world," (Jung 1950b/1959 paras 631, 664) who is joined inextricably to Sakti, his emanations (L. Stein 2013, 185)? The disciples dancing around the center point of Christ, devoting their libido to him as the axis, the nub of presence, find mirrored their subjective consciousness and their potential wholeness and that makes them visible to themselves and others. At the same time their concentration of libido on the center brings to visibility, into nearness, this origin point, Christ. In Jung's vocabulary, ego mirrors Self and Self mirrors ego. Thus each penetrates the other in mutual recognition, indeed, in joy and enhances their coming into being. The center shows itself, coming into visibility by our devotion to it and we, the disciples, come into visibility by the center seeing us (Jung 1954/1958, paras 418, 424, 427; see also above, 13-14).

Meaning Once Again

We are back to the question of meaning. The disciples come into fuller being and the center itself shows its fuller presence. Energy moves back and forth from each to each. Such movement of energy is what we as clinicians track in analytical sessions and try to describe in theory (e.g. Fordham's deintegration and reintegration of the self, Bedi's description of transformation in collective, historical periods in cultural life) (Bedi 2013, 108-120).

Such exchanging of recognition is native to soul's intermediate position reflecting interpenetration of ego and Self in unfolding of personal individuation, and in becoming conscious of one's contribution to and honoring of the whole which is called God or what we name in place of God.

My point is that we are speaking here of growth of psyche, function and role of soul, and the elusive animating breath of spirit which is at once personal, and a collective dimension in which we live (the "spirit of the depths"). Yet all three terms – psyche, soul, spirit – often used interchangeably and other times defined separately – all together indicate not only the vital interchanges on the human level but beyond themselves to the something more of reality, reality itself. That is where the word God appears. Are numinous experiences indications of our meaning–making of symbols, expressing human imagination and ingenuity? Or are they also pointing to meaning existing independently, self-subsistent, showing itself? Jung acknowledges the independence of this spirit revealing itself: "the spirit is quite capable of staging its own manifestations spontaneously" (Jung 1948/1959, para 395). Do we have eyes to see it and ears to hear and stomachs to take the impact of its thereness, pressing toward us to be not just acknowleged but loved?

Jung's psychology implicitly urges our living aligned with Self. But often Self and ego conflict, as I have said above. What to do with Self that opposes ego life: "activity of self may not be in service of the ego but will be in service of the whole, the totality of the psyche" (McAlister 2014, 167). Activity of the ego may press its urgency over the movements of Self perspective. Nonetheless, such aligning can be achieved even when facing terminal diagnosis of illness that will cut our life short (see Ulanov 1994; see Ulanov 1996, 173-178). Such alignment makes vivid the difference between meaningful suffering and suffering as utter waste.

To receive a communication of the meaning related to a traumatic happening is to be alerted to something unknown emerging into living, an experience of an archetypal resonance that links us into images in human history. Not only are we not then alone, isolated, but part of human family; not only do we register with liveliness the correspondence of archetypal image with our personal image, but sometimes we are also redeemed from traumatic wounding.

Example

An example is a sense of liberation felt by a late middle-age man from a lifetime of inferiority and loss of father support. Born with retracted toes, so bent from birth he failed even to start to be the athlete his father projected into him. His father longed to see his son star in one of the stadium filled sports of their small university town. This only son would be the hero for the father, compensating his father's felt inferiority as lower class failure to earn more for his disapproving wife. He even tried to make the son's curved toes straighten despite the boy's humiliation when this failed.

Losing his father's endorsement contributed to the man's adult life swirling into addiction, secret sexual acting out that put his successful persona functioning at risk. He consciously settled for dissociation – keeping his life in separate compartments. His image for this resolve emerged in the course of our work. He imaginatively gathered the dissociated parts finally together into a line of train cars at his town's small railroad station, a place he loved to visit as a boy. He chose not to link up the cars. He desired to leave them unlinked. The train looked like it could start and go somewhere, but the cars remained unlinked.

I saw in my countertransference my enthusiasm that the train could start now and conduct his travels, and, like his father, I imagined his finding a path to fulfill. I learned otherwise, to respect his choice to leave space between the cars so they could sit there in the station, look like a train, but remain still, not going anywhere. I often mused on this acceptance of space to be, a secret interval maintained to protect or assert his refusal to get on anybody's train, but instead to stay in being with his own construction, to find and dwell in being.

Then his workplace gave him a sabbatical and he took a trip abroad. By chance, he came upon a large mosaic in the Cupola of a Florence church of "Christ as Judge" – potent, all knowing, presiding as God, not the suffering broken Christ on the cross. In this exalted position Christ displayed hooked toes, almost like talons, just like the man's own. He sent me a postcard of this picturing of God as not now Son of the Father but of the Father in the Son, showing the Son fulfilling the Father's might and glory (Firenze Battistero DI S. Giovanni, Mosaic of the Cupola (13th century) Christ Judge). He penned these words on his postcard: "I was pleased to see God has "clawed" feet too!" When we resumed analysis he quipped that what is good enough for God is good enough for me. I felt in the silence that followed love he felt for his actual self, able now to carry the father wound, not to be defined by it. Love for his real self to be, not to go and do but to be.

6. Spiritual Elements in Clinical Work

To look into spiritual elements in clinical work is to point to the 'something more' that comes through the work and that undergirds it. Practicing analysts all know about this added factor. We call it different names. Some of us feel strongly not to get into religious matters, or even spiritual ones, though spirituality is generally more acceptable. I understand this antipathy to religion, expressed as firm avoidance of the whole topic, as traceable to either early bad experiences of religion – a dominating structure demanding compliance imposed on a child's mind at the expense of free hearted thinking guided by curiosity. Or, it may be due simply to lack of any religious exposure so one would not really know where to begin to see links to the transcendent. But something is there, witness the flourishing association of Buddhist practices of meditation with psychoanalysis. That testifies to truth of Buddhism but also offers a different route into spiritual matters seemingly uncontaminated with fundamentalistic histories associated with religion. Fanaticism comes in all garbs, but it is remarkable that the terrorism rampant in our 21st century adopts a religious persona and requires an insistent reference to a transcendent God as justification for its violences.

Something More (Again)

Religion, in contrast to spirituality, is more embodied in practices of belonging to communities of participants, of emphasis on works toward and with others, and on texts and Scriptures of inherited tradition in which one finds space freely to explore and consent in prayer and ritual. Spirituality appears less defined and confined but brings with it its own dangers of being less tethered to the grounded, embodied life here and now. Hence one can waft above the conflicts and inevitable tensions of everyday life, at the least lacking red-blooded engagement, and at the worst floating away or becoming unhinged.

Whatever place we find ourselves, which can shift over decades, as analysts there is a shared sense of something more going on when treatment succeeds. Analysands find their ways in linking this life to some bigger life. When I use the word spiritual 'elements' I mean something elementary, basic, a rudiment, a building block. I have written about this before, but feel impelled to do so again, describing the elements, not in an exhaustive way, but a varied way from before (see Ulanov 1996b). The saints, whatever tradition, tell us again and again, that however we describe God, or what we put in place of God, is never grasped in our names but always lives beyond them and before them. Nicholas of Cusa says God is simplicity, neither being nor nonbeing but both before and beyond. (Nicholas of Cusa 1997, 211, 212, 213).

It behooves us as clinicians with the care of others in our work to be in conversation with this 'something more' because it influences our ability to see, hear, listen, perceive what is going on at the level of what makes living possible, not just to survive awful things that happen to people, but to thrive, with happiness in being alive. It adds to what the analysand reaches in analysis the clearer we are – not with conclusions – but in recognizing, at least to ourselves, the quiddity (*quidditas*), the whatness to which we feel we belong. From that whatness proceed our methods of doing analysis, and understanding how we are done by it. We can also read in each other's work those elements shining through their theories.

Tracking the Tiger

Bion saying that "Psycho-analysis is just a stripe on the coat of the tiger" and that we hope one day to meet the tiger, warms the heart and seems so apt about the presence of the something more in analytical sessions (Bion 1991). Elusive, even threatening, but ultimately there, this "tiger" seems to confirm what we are doing, or trying to. Maybe better put, it is doing us. In tracking the tiger, what are some of the spiritual elements?

Dead Parts

I think first and foremost of looking into, going into, dead parts of oneself, to the hell of places where all is lost and the experience of lostness is itself lost. We thaw out what has been frozen into immobility by warm-blooded attention. One patient after she felt she was not kept in the analyst's mind, but forgotten, not remembered, dreamt throwing ice cubes at the analyst, with intent to hurt. The dream pictures shards of frozen feeling (the dreamer's association) now accessible and gathered into an aim of protest, something she had never done in the past relationship with her mother. Now she felt deeply her loss and her destructiveness, and realized she felt she was not ever in the mind of her mother. We might surmise from the youngness, the childlike quality of the image of throwing ice-cubes to hurt the analyst that this suffering extends all the way into her childhood as well as into the present relationship with the analyst. This trip to hell and back reinstalls a bit of her agency as a person. Feeling a subject in her own right makes it possible not just to bear her suffering, but also to protest it and register her desire to be held in mind by another, to be validated. A kind of faith is implicit in analysis that we will grow if we try to connect to dead parts of ourselves, even unacceptable experiences. We might say our inner recognition provides psychic ground for a sense of justice to others.

Another example illustrates the preciousness of feeling one has enlivening agency and shows how it spreads into the world more space to be, to act with thought and feeling. We do not usually know how effective our changing is on others. Personal recovery can go aways to redeem others who know nothing about our change but receive its fruit. This analysand showed great distress in what she called her failure as actor to fulfill the emotional moment in the drama when the character she portrayed asserted her betraying action to force the other character, a medical doctor, to admit her husband into the experimental program which he had been denied, but which might save his life.

The previous rehearsal of this scene had gone very well. What happened in the performance? She missed it, she said. She could not summon her full self to speak these lines of destructive/constructive resolve. It lacked truth, she said; and she made the mistake of pushing herself to reach full embodiment of truthfulness; that only made it worse. She felt this failure keenly. And it happened again in her next performance!

A good deal of digging unearthed an unguessed connection between this lack of authenticity in her acting and her ongoing grief that had surfaced in the recent months of analysis about nonrelation with her father. Caught in his conflicts, masked by his steady drinking during her growing-up years, she had, as she put it, never had a father, no time ever with him as a daughter learning from her father about truth, how to be in the world, how to work, present oneself, how to be and do anything. Immediately returning home from work he took his evening drink(s); I had to perform to get his attention, she said. Her phobia of drunks and drug addicts on the city street terrified her; she saw them as people who had let go of their minds, lost their lives. Suddenly a connection emerged with her recent months of lamentation about having no real father. He seemed to her a lost soul like the men on the streets, not there, though covered up by rigid rule-based adherence to religion.

All this perception and grieving came to a head due to a sudden shocking family death and her father's seeming obliviousness of how she, too, had suffered greatly. He appeared to expect her to drop her life with its obligations to children, husband and work to tend to his upset as the only important factor. Although she gave him much attention and time, she felt unable to speak up to him about his not crediting her loss and grief, or seeming to care much about her in any way. She justified her not speaking to him about this erasure by saying she did not want to hurt him; she felt it would make no difference; she feared he would attack her for challenging his behavior. We muddled along.

To our mutual surprise in a session it became unavoidably and completely clear she could not speak truthfully in her acting because she was not speaking truthfully from her self to her father. There it was, the link. It took some time for her to decide to speak up and she did, feeling she must be true to herself, though she met with her father's denial, and dismissive attack. Nonetheless her tongue in acting was unlocked, her heart flowed again into her performance and she fulfilled an authentic role. It changed her and her audiences, though it did not change her parent. Who knows how many people were reached by effective communication of truth in the drama she was portraying? We do not, or not usually, know effects of our own growth on other people. The justification does not lie in the results but in the willingness to do one's part, one's true part, to respond to an imperative addressed to our soul.

Individual/Collective

A second element close on to refinding one's subjectness – that one has not been erased by violence or neglect, but has power to vote and the courage to execute it – is consciousness of the inextricable connection between the individual and collective, the personal and social. What we do destructively to self or other in action or attitude is what also gets done on a mass level. Madness knows no borders. The soul that lives in each of us contributes to or subtracts from the spirit in which we all dwell. If I make a part of me dead, cut it off, segregate it from the parts of me that remain alive inside, whether out of pain of feeling the hurt of that part, or out of fear of becoming murderous if I keep that part alive, I put into the shared existence with others a deadening of fellow feeling that binds us into instinctive obedience to law.

That interior deadening makes a hole in the cultural matrix by refusing to recognize and hold to what is collectively understood as unacceptable, that must not be done, thus weakening a safety barrier that guards against wanton destructiveness. I weaken the shared trust that such and such is wrong. The one who gets infected by that increased license is usually the one among us least defended, mentally vulnerable, if not ill. He is the one who makes a video of himself with automatic weapons in both hands to gun people down and then goes out onto Virginia Tech campus and does just that – heedlessly, profligately shooting students and faculty.

If I look into the greed underlying my inferiority complex – that I feel unable because I want everything and I want everything because I feel so unable – and consciously engage my greedy impulses to stuff into me food or money or shopping sprees or getting power over others, surpassing my need and the object's ability to give, this hard painful work yields more inner space. My capacities expand to assimilate, initiate, risk diverse options. I add that increased capacity into the cultural milieu, making more oxygen for all of us. Similarly, if I acknowledge the grief I fear will take me out to sea because of the loss of the beloved object, of the goodness in my life, if I allow awareness of that dark lamenting, who knows but some song, some poetry, like Orpheus, will emerge from it.

Our particular part in our particular contexts cannot be discarded without subtracting from the larger cultural coherence. We must find a place for our specificity in relation to the whole as that is the nexus point to perceive universal order. We profit from each other's contributions to the atmosphere in which we all live our shared existence. We feel gratitude, indebtedness to others for what they carry, suffer and work on to make into insight into its meaning. Their living experiences increase the spirit that animates the world and all of us prosper.

Right away, however, comes to mind experiences of the bad, bad happenings that never resolve – a friendship broken off and refusal to work through the rupture together so that one is left not even wishing the other well. Or an eruption of predatory sexual attraction and rage break out when it is not received and then follows abusive verbal attack. Despite no external justification for such behavior, the enraged abuser refuses to look into this chthonic eruption and find what of value may be lurking in its berserker display. Or we are felled by horror-filled collective genocide, forced marches, starvation campaigns, rape camps, events so repellent and huge, we cannot digest nor imagine how ever to make amends. What to do with such unacceptable experiences that inflict hell on us!

The Really Bad

Here a third spiritual element has to do with bad that exceeds our comprehension or ability to assimilate and heal. These experiences remain bad; they are bad experiences, experiences of the bad. I would suggest they, too, get a seat at the table and should not be buried alive, nor ignored, nor cut out of our collective historical records, or family narratives (Davoine and Gaudilliere 2004). Hidden, they act like grenades within a self or a family or a social unit, with all the consequent anxiety. Will someone inadvertently pull the pin? Or, will the grenade just lying there poison the entire system? Or sink us like a stone in our gut?

Acknowledgement of the bad is a form of defense against being victimized again by it. Through words, images, we make a place for it at the table. But, its place at the table is marked as unworthy, as ignominy. The bad gets a seat at the table as the bad; the place-card names it as the unacceptable. That is its place, where it belongs. Such admission keeps us real – neither obsessively going over and over, for years, a bad experience, nor ignoring it, often with a pill to sedate us; nor in a grudge to keep poking it like a sore tooth, spreading its infection through our body and into the cultural body. We give the bad a place but label it as disgrace, infamy. We do not get rid of the bad, but we do not indulge it either. It has its restricted place so we do not go on getting contaminated by its residue. We give trauma some room, restricted and labeled, confined, instead of our living in it. We carry trauma in our awareness of it, but do not fuel its ongoing life. We recognize it as intolerable, improper, dishonorable.

Scraps Again

A fourth spiritual element (the first three being going into hell of dead places, accepting the connection of personal and collective life, accepting the place of the unacceptable) deserves emphasis because of its tendril-like connection to other spiritual elements, describing a sort of network. By scraps I mean two kinds of things – the bits and pieces of our personal life, their contexts in specific neighborhood, city, or countryside, and in our notable culture and even time in history. I also mean how scraps communicate their importance to us through odd image, imperative body impulse, sly hint, fugitive thought, hunch, that nudge off the main road onto a bypath that takes us to what we must confront or heal (Ulanov 2013/2014, 231-232).

Scraps are bits, grains, traces, morsels, often scrapped, discarded, tossed, because seemingly so trivial and accidental. But there lurk creative seeds, the decisive dream detail that opens the dream's entire meaning, the idiosyncratic accent in an active imagination that confirms its realness. Archetypal images do not resonate with enlivening effects until made personal and what makes them personal are scraps of us that like a small key open to a scope of understanding. In Goethe's *Faust* the scrap plays a pivotal role: Mephistopheles says, "Here, take this key." Faust says, "That little thing." Mephistopheles says, "Take hold of it and don't underrate it.... This key will nose out the way for you. Follow its lead. It'll conduct you to the Mothers" (cited in Edinger 1990, 55.) We create out of scraps, our attention caught by a glimmer of something. Following its gleam, like the old camp-side song, we sing our way toward light. Scraps link to larger coincidences through which we register an assemblage of meaning.

As analysts we learn to pay attention to these chance appearances in the analysand's material and in our response to them; they unveil the collective unconscious that produces them and our awareness of the link between personal and collective builds. They bring to mind the Cabiri in Jung's *Red Book* (Jung 2009, 320-321; see also Ulanov 2013, 58-59). Scraps are important, if not pivotal, indicating this person's unique process of individuation: "the cure ought to grow naturally out of the patient himself (Jaffé 1963, 131).

Scraps, however, stay scraps, hints, not evolved theses with reasoned argument, but accidents, odd congruences that reveal a possibility, not a full knowledge. Attention to scraps means consent to not-knowing, an emptiness not full up with preparedness, certain what to do, believe, say. Thus we always find we are among those called the spiritually poor, not in possession of spiritual objects but ready to see the nod, get the hint, hear the pause in spoken words.

Tutored by scraps, we respond to whatever appears in emptiness. Response can be yes or no, yea or nay, not meek compliance nor angry repudiation, but engaging the object and registering one's subjectness. Spiritual life is not a smorgasbord where we get to choose, oh some of this and none of that, and maybe a little extra of that desert over there. Scraps alert us that we do not know yet point to what arrives; response takes what is offered, or freely responds with our personal nay.

Such free responding recalls the willingness that marks the soul. Soul life expresses itself in readiness. We go forth to the other; we want the connection. Desire fuels our longing for engagement of mutual recognition and enhancement – with unknown parts of our self, with the idiosyncratic suchness of the other, with the author of all that is. Soul life is marked by surprise, refreshment, animation. Soul life may lead to full-bodied answer where all the functions of thinking, feeling, sensing, intuiting interpenetrate. Soul life can lead us beyond ourselves. On the way to that giving-over, two different and interconnected modes of consciousness – child and adult – come into steady play.

Modes of Consciousness

Matisse captures the mode of child consciousness that is necessary for painting. It includes unconscious processes, one's particular world, valor, and the binding of love: "Having ... emptied my mind of all preconceived ideas, I traced this preliminary outline with a hand completely given over to my unconscious sensations.... The effort to see things without distortion takes something very like courage ... the artist has to look at everything as though he saw it for the first time: he has to look at life as he did when he was a child and, if he loses that faculty, he cannot express himself in an original, that is, a personal way.... The artist ... gradually assimilates the external world within himself....

Great love is needed to achieve this effect" (Flamm 1978, 151, 148-9; cited in Ulanov 2001a, 65).

Child consciousness is free of preconceptions, shoulds and should-nots; it uses that soul willingness to see what is there and what is not there and to respond to it, make something of it. It includes wonder, beholding, concentrated attention in the moment. Scraps command such attention; we notice those accidents where something different comes into view, or a body response says, yes, follow this. Child consciousness conveys its mythological nature and is to be differentiated from literal childhood, of which Jung says (his italics), "*The childish is unfruitful, what is to come to him already has been engendered and already withered. It does not live onward*" (Jung 2009, 234, 229, n3). In contrast, the child motif "compensates the onesidedness of consciousness and paves the way for the future development of the personality. In conflict the child may symbolize the uniting of opposites: "It anticipates the self, which is produced through the synthesis of the conscious and unconscious elements of the personality." (ibid, 234, n 58).

What I have called inaugural images that originate as a soul spark within us elicit that child mode of immediate attentiveness. A patient confided that the stepfather who interfered with her sexually, whom she hated for it, was also the one who, earlier, when she was a small girl, taught her not to be afraid of the dark and especially not to fear the insects and swamp creatures that came out in the night in her native South. Hence she grew up with abiding interest in bugs, snakes, even crocodiles, for which she was grateful to him. The child wonder in her survived intact his later sexual depredations.

Winnicott finds that the destruction we learn to use through the use of the object that opens the world to us still does not use up all our destructiveness (Winnicott 1969/1989, 232, 245; see also Winnicott 1971, chapter 6; see also Winnicott, 1986, 117-118; see also Ulanov 2001a, 116-119, 123, 147). That leftover destructiveness falls into our unconscious where it stirs creative imagination. We thus expand into the capacity imaginatively to destroy the painting we love and that makes the loving all the more steady and precious (Winnicott 1986, 90; see also Ulanov 2001a, 65). Such imaginative use of destructiveness, keeps a child pattern of original perception continuing into adult life.

I understand this unconscious imaginative destructiveness as if windshield wipers that sweep away accumulated judgments, projections, stereotypes, preconceptions, interpretations so that we can perceive daily life in ever new ways. We open to diversity. Our options widen. We become "equipped to see everything in a fresh way, to be creative in every detail of living" (Winnicott 1970, 41; see also Ulanov 2001a, 117 and 107-124). Even finding a place for unacceptable experiences that never get resolved but cease to hold us hostage, even those widen our capacities to house the forces of living, to endure a surplus of perception.

What makes this child consciousness different from its first appearance in childhood is that we are already adult and hence have with it, even simultaneously at times, adult capacities to observe, reflect, differentiate, discern, deconstruct, analyse into component parts the wonder that has knocked us flat before the object inspiring it. A patient once brought a picture from a fashion magazine of an utterly beautiful model, gorgeous in silken clothes, of glowing skin, shining hair and the poised, unselfconscious gracefulness of an animal. Her eyes and the look in them brought as well a subdued ferocity as if a wild animal, yet she was definitely a person with a mind and intent. The man said, this my anima, using Jung's name for the feminine image that quickens a man's soul, animating his life. She was that for sure but also as if from both animal world and spiritual beyond. He needed to use his adult mind to look into and analyze all that drew him in order to admit these powers into consciousness, not to snuff them but to protect against being swung right out of existence to escape to an island with her. The movie "Splash" portrayed a man so captivated he quit his life on land to join his mermaid living under the sea.

Qualities of child consciousness bring uninhibited uninterfered with immediacy. Saints at the apex of spiritual development feel that mediators of priest, sacrament, or doctrine are no longer the principal means to be in touch with their God. God is near, here, now. Qualities of adult consciousness bring perspective, context, anchoring in traditions of human wisdom that enable us to shape our soul willingness into sustained practices of devotion or service. Such qualities make for restraint in facing urgent impulse, to channel it, consider where it is useful, thus bringing into awareness capacity for practical wisdom. We construct attitudes toward untamed instincts to cultivate their energies and preside over them even when faced with rage. Qualities of adult consciousness allow for consideration of our affect. We can make a space between its urgencies of desire and our choice for action or non-action Thus we accrue self-discipline that includes foresight, even strategy of the best way to proceed. With lucid intelligence we can see beyond immediate satisfaction through good counsel and discernment. Adult qualities bring consultation and communication with others, admitting the rare into conversation, chastening reckless abandonment to the moment with the space-making of tradition, and time-making of present knowledge and perspective.

We need both modes of child and adult consciousness. Dangers of extremes can infect both – either undiscriminating innocence that easily gets smashed, or over-thinking that can indulge shrewdness into crafty manipulation of others. Both modes turn up in clinical work, in the analyst and in the analysand.

Inaugural Images (Again), Psychoanalytic Theories and God-Images

It is the capacity for child wonder that sees the soul's spark nestled in the raw material of us – the stuff of our ordinary, familiar life with its hidden treasure yet to be discovered. The sparks set off ignition, even explosions. Our capacity for beholding notices those sparks, responds with curiosity, even fear, yet also aggression to inquire, perceive what is going on here. As we catch sight of these sparks, Jung's *scintillae* in the dark of the unconscious like fireflies in the night, and string them together in reflection, they describe a path along which an image may appear. That image inaugurates for us a meeting with 'something more,' a point of beginning, like the elemental point in geometry that expands to a line, a plane, then to a solid which means a manifestation of psychic reality projected into external reality that allows us to deal more effectively with it. (Edinger 1995, 57-58)

Physicists' hypothesis of Higgs Boson particle, called the 'God particle' because "it is responsible ... for the masses of all elementary particles" is not itself seen but initiates being, incarnating mass in the commonplace world, advancing our knowledge of laws of nature and the extensive effects of such knowledge (Randall 2011, 284-285; see also Randall 2013, 1-4, 38-40). Similarly, the image inspired by soul sparks appearing and reappearing in scraps of our lives, has psychic reality that may initiate incarnating – giving mass to, embodiment of – a guiding path.

The life force in such images unfolds in theories we clinicians develop about how the psyche works and what promotes healing. I mentioned earlier examples but here are a few in addition. Often there may be more than one such luminous image of the supreme good in an analyst's theory--Klein's 'good breast,' Loewald's 'loving the truth of his patient's psyche,' Winnicott's 'play,' Sechahaye's 'symbolic reality,' Bollas' 'idiom' and Jung at the end of his life, and what he came to at the end of *The Red Book* as his hard won solution to the split between intimacy with another and freedom: 'Love' (Jung 2009, 356 and Jaffé 1963, 325).

These images of the ultimate good sustain us in clinical work; indeed they represent what symbolizes the good existing in life, as well as our trust we can connect with it. This symbol points to something more that exists far outside us, not only outside our ego but beyond our psyche too. And this goodness or what it symbolizes as the infinite, the ultimately precious, exists deep inside us, thus indicating mutual origins: what is at the center of reality also dwells at the center of us.

Some clinicians might hold psyche as the God-image, where the buck stops, the source of all configurations of the good, of truth, of God. Jung is ambiguous on this point, saying all we can know are our God-images which we must believe convey the real God. Yet also when he says such numinous and religious images come through the psyche, indeed through the psychoid 'level' of the psyche, Jung does not mean what they represent is psychic. Rather, we are only able to point to where the numinous appears: "This transcendent nature of all experience does not mean that the transcendent realities are also psychic; the physicist does not believe the transcendental reality represented by his psychic model is also psychic. He calls it *matter,* and in the same way the psychologist in no wise attributes a psychic nature to his images or archetypes. He calls them 'psychoids' and is convinced that they represent transcendental realities ... *a conviction one cannot avoid*" (Jung 1954/1976, para 1538).

Ricoeur makes the same point, that of course we reify our intimations of the source of religious experience. The experience is overwhelming and convincing. Jung agrees saying, "it is the gift of the Holy Spirit ... an immediate presence, often terrifying and in no degree subject to our choice" (ibid). I see the God-image made up of personal details that particularize our lives, cultural contexts that locate us, traditions of wisdom that feed us, and the something more we respond to: a there there that cannot be identified with any item, idea, symbolic imagining of the here here. Religious life includes the pattern Ricoeur recognizes, of reifying our images and dereifying them, of, in zeal and overwhelm, identifying our image of God with God and disidentifying any image with the mystery that authors such vision. We live the paradox of creating the image that finds us and finding an image that arrives from its own source that far exceeds our constructions. We know we did not invent it. We help create the image we find and feel it creates us in its finding us (see Ulanov 2012/2015, 168-169; see also 2008/2014, 164f, 173, 175; see also 2001a, 10, 11, 20-26, 62-64, 97-99,105-106; see also Ulanov and Ulanov 1991/1999, 59-72).

Of pivotal importance is the mutual penetrating of the God-image and the ego of consciousness: "formations of the God-image ... run parallel with changes in human consciousness, though one would be at a loss to say which is the cause of the other. The God-image is not something *invented*, it is an *experience* that comes upon man spontaneously.... The unconscious God-image can therefore alter the state of consciousness, just as the latter can modify the God-image once it has become conscious" (Jung 1959, para 303).

The Psychoid

Jung also writes that where the image finds us is where it simply appears, not where it originates. He again mentions the psychoid as a 'place' where such an image turns up, here making it synonymous with the soul: "One cannot reduce its origin to that place: "When I say, 'Here is the source,' I only mean the spot where the water becomes visible.... A metaphysical being does not as a rule speak through the telephone to you; it usually communicates with man through the medium of the soul, in other words, the unconscious, or rather through its transcendental 'psychoid' basis" (Jung 1956-57/1956, para 1586).

We are returned here to experience of psychoid quality of unconscious raising the issue of meaning. Did my analysand and I create the meaning of dwelling together in the unraveling of our accustomed roles of patient/doctor who know and can reflect on what is happening, but now are just dwelling in a larger time in space or space in time, being there, not knowing about it? Did we invent the meaning of deep trustworthiness in the work we engaged in together? Or was that meaning bestowed on us, blessing us? Or is it both?

In such moments of living in the wholeness of the whole, we glimpse meaning in performing our service to it, penetrated by its grant of meaningfulness to us. Even in unacceptable suffering we are not left alone. Something bigger enfolds us in a larger circumference. We feel under regard. Meaning matters, our part matters; it helps make up the whole. The soul completes addition; we are added into the center of what is, from the center of what we are. With such sums, some of us, Jung included, call these inaugural images that grow substantial in our theories about meaning that matters, God-images (Ulanov and Ulanov 1991/1999, chapter 2; see also Ulanov 2001a, 21-36). The excursus of Chapter 7 offers an example of a big God-image of Nicholas of Cusa. He experiences this image connecting him to God, and his experience impacts Jung's theory.

7. Excursus: Coincidence of Opposites – Nicholas of Cusa and C. G. Jung

Jung's Style

With his astonishing range of knowledge Jung refers to Nicholas of Cusa of the 15th century whom he quoted in Latin and translated to borrow the perception of coincidence of opposites to describe God. Jung can be criticized for his somewhat fast and loose style of appropriating another's concept for his own purposes, failing to give it accurate definition in the original author's thinking (Brooks 2011, 491-492, 497; see also Bright 2014, 81). Jung can thus distort the term's meaning.

When first writing about Jung' s ideas I remember fashioning 'symbolic concept' to cite his name for psychic complexes (Ulanov 1971, 24). That strategy combined symbol, that opens to unknown and maybe unknowable reaches, with concept, to designate theoretical idea. Jung's is not a conceptual system, proceeding in linear reasoning, but instead offers descriptions full of affect, piling up of images that express emotion mixed with thought, body senses along with intuitive leaps. His writing circles round and round a point until its meaning emerges, a method some readers find off-putting. Other readers find his style illumining because close to actual living, where all our faculties mix up with each other to produce impact through an encompassing impression from which we then must dig ourselves out to gain clarity. Jung derived his terms from life – shadow from dreams of being chased by penumbral figures, persona from masks we don in public through which our souls resound like actors of ancient Greece, anima/animus from the other who enlivens us sexually and spiritually in our connection to reality, Self like a bigger expanse, different from, yet intimately involved with ego, as if two centers of consciousness inhabit us.

In Jung's use of Nicholas of Cusa's terms there is a misuse and a flash of insight, both (a coincidence of opposites). Jung says Nicholas identifies the *coincidentia oppositorum* with God (Jung 1946/1954, para 537). That is incorrect and distorts Nicholas' meaning. But in the same paragraph Jung cites Nicholas to say, "God is above the opposites" which is accurate rendition, translating the Latin to read in Nicholas' words, "Beyond this coincidence of creating and being created art Thou God" (ibid).

God-Image

Retrieving accurate use of Nicolas' terms clarifies the large meaning of coincidence of opposites and the God it points to. It also, I suggest, deepens Jung's insights and solves a problem that wrestled Jung as he wrestled it. But first let us look at coincidence of opposites as a powerful God-image for Nicholas that leads to his final illumination at the end of his life, an even fuller God-image that delivered him into happiness. Peter, his secretary, is reported to say of Nicholas' final writing, *The Summit of Contemplation*, "I find you more relaxed and joyous as if you had discovered some great thing.... What new discovery has come to you in your meditation during these Paschal [Easter] days.... What are you seeking?" And Nicholas replies "You speak correctly.... I am seeking *what*." (Nicholas of Cusa 1997, 293). Peter asks, Do you believe it can be found? And Nicholas answers "Certainly.... *Posse* Itself, without which nothing whatever can be ... this is the *What* ... Whatness itself, without which nothing at all can be. And it is this contemplation that has occupied my thoughts with great delight during these holy days" (ibid, 294). "The clearer the truth is the easier it is. I once thought it could be found better in darkness. But of great power is the truth in which *Posse* Itself shines brightly. Indeed it shouts in the streets, as you have read in my tract *On the Ignorant*" (ibid, 295). Nicholas of Cusa's final image for God, which only God can be, is possibility, "Can-Is," "Can-That Is," "Can-Itself: the *quiddity* itself without which nothing can be" (ibid, 58, 339, 340).

A God-image alive for its holder connects to the reality of God to which it points symbolically. For Nicholas God is this *Possest*; through this image, Nicholas sees the center and author of reality and describes it: "'Can' beyond, antecedent to, behind, and present in all that 'is' " (ibid, 340). God is not any symbol. No name, no image, no imagining, no conceptualizing, no reasoning, no thinking, no beyond senses, no intellect, no inward self can define God. God is incomprehensible, unthinkable, beyond knowing and not knowing, beyond unity and otherness, beginnings and endings, now and then, particular and universal, creating and being created, even being and non-being; God transcends all opposites.

The only route for us creatures is to learn our ignorance – that we cannot know God. And, *mirabile dictu,* coincidence of opposites is the means and the method of perceiving, with tremendous emotion and personal feeling of love, the central whatness, the power to be "*Posse-ipsum* (can itself, having power itself, possibility itself"; "Can-Itself" is God "the actuality of potency" (ibid 339, 340) present in all things, including us, because God knows us and notices us.

Unlike many theologians (contra Jung's description of Nicholas as philospher (Jung 1946/1954, para 537), Nicholas writes passionately full of feeling. In so far as this is philosophy, Nicholas says, it is such as "filled with wonder ... more as *therapeia* and as *cura animarum* than as *logica*" (Nicholas of Cusa 1997, 17). His works, especially the late ones – *On The Summit of Contemplation, On The Vision of God, On Seeking God, Dialogue On The Hidden God*

– read more like prayers than systematic tracts. He is in conversation with God. He bursts out with his desire and its fulfillment, saying "I run forth" (ibid, 40, 218, 225, 230); "to race after God from an ardent wondering" (ibid, 42, 228); "truth shouts in the streets," (ibid, 295); our mind exists "to run toward" *Posse* (ibid, 67, 301, 303), (not unlike Jung emphasizing the purpose of human life is consciousness, the creature's gift to creator). Nicholas says, "we must leap beyond simple likeness" (ibid, 102); "one leaps across every knowledge" (ibid, 244); "I must leap beyond every seminal power ... and in the cloud I find a most astonishing power" (ibid, 245). And to us, Nicholas says, "you will marvel," (ibid, 48, 236), pointing to God as "the mind's most delectable food," (ibid, 281), as "O fountain of riches" (ibid, 266). To us, again, Nicholas says, "our intellectual spirit has the power of fire in it ... to glow and spring up in flame" (ibid, 228); and then offers this astounding insight: "whatever we seem to project into the form of God is in fact God's gift to us" (ibid, 49, 242).[10] He says of God, "O God who are goodness itself" (ibid, 283); "one cannot know God's truth, which is incomprehensible, except by leaping across the image ... seeing the truth is seeing through and beyond the image" (ibid, 31, 339).

Nicholas, not unlike Jung, is a very busy professional of standing in the world and a passionate reacher to truth, more affective than conceptual, though also very erudite, for example, using mathematics as his analogy to describe the infinite itself. After receiving his new and complete revelation, about the power to be, the "*Posse* ipsum ... Self-Subsistent in all things, the "Essence in Itself" (ibid, 340), he finds intimations of his powerful image of "Can-Is" in others' works. His research also shows him a gradual unfolding toward this vision of God in his own prior work in sermons and in his famous treatise "On Learned Ignorance."

10. I add this fifth function of projection to the four others I have written about elsewhere (Ulanov 2001a, 97-106). The radicality of Nicholas' assertion exposes projection not as distortion of reality by the imposition of subjective contents upon it, but a meeting place with reality, that is, reality named God. In this kind of projection, meeting occurs between and within one's subjectivity with ultimate reality in the specific fashion of our projection.

Coincidence of Opposites

But let us get to the coincidence of opposites. This is not God. The opposites coincide in God; God encompasses them; they reside in God, showing a unity of contraries that fall together disclosing how God works and how humans can approach God. God precedes all contradictories, opposites, distinctions (see the excellent introduction and glossary of translator H. Lawrence Bond, ibid, 45, 336). The coincidence is a unity of all opposites without mingling, mixing, fusing them, nor diminishing their separate entities. But their differentiated state yields to the greater surround of harmony in God.

Yet it is not quite true even to say coincidence of opposites reside in God because there is nothing that can be said about God who is so beyond our comprehension, living within the wall or on the other side of the wall surrounding paradise. Rather, the coincidence of opposites is the door to the wall around paradise; it is our way of conceiving God – that God enfolds all things in Godself. Coincidence of opposites is the method of thinking of God – that God is infinite unity in which all diversity resides. Yet, we must realize all the time nothing we say or think or image approaches God (ibid, 238). We best seek fulfillment of our desire for God in the immediate reality of our ignorance – for God is beyond all our categories of knowing. Our ignorance becomes learned. The coincidence of opposites brings us nearer to God.

Coincidence of opposites is the door to the wall within which God lives. It is the way God manifests in the world though God lives on the other side of the wall marking off earthly life from paradise where God dwells. We find no other way of approaching God than this door. For the coincidence of opposites confounds all our human ways of knowing, including images (although Nicholas uses many – painter, face, mirror, nut tree, clock, mathematics, our sight – while denying their efficacy to speak of God – coincidence!) (ibid, 235, 241-245). He says of his God-image: "I have discovered that the place where you are found unveiled is girded about with the coincidence of contradictories. This is the wall of paradise, and it is there in paradise that you reside. Thus, it is the other side of the coincidence of contradictories that you will be able to be seen and nowhere on this side." (ibid, 252; see also 254). The bafflement of ways of knowing that coincidence of opposites evokes in us brings us beyond human categories of space, time, causality. We apprehend our ignorance and go through the door to seeing God as Possibility in all things, the essential whatness of anything that is. The allness of God penetrates our ignorance.

Five Parallels Between Jung and Nicholas of Cusa

Some close parallels suggest themselves between the thought of Jung and Nicholas of Cusa. Because discussing the psychoid quality of the unconscious is to experience its impact, I have found writing about it slow going, always susceptible to dissolution. One is right away in the midst of coincidence of opposites, for example, registering that physical and psychical are not qualities of two separate things but two sides of the same moment or content of thought or event, let alone all the other opposites that now coincide. It is as if one is a fish trying to describe the water one swims in without just being taken off into its currents. I can feel my discrete thoughts and feelings dissolving as I am trying to bring them to crisp clarity. So I will list here these connections between Jung's and Nicholas' thought in summary fashion, before they swim away.

1. To begin with, for Jung psychoid quality of the unconscious annuls our ego ways of knowing with its binary differentiations. We are permeated by awareness that we lose those usual points of reference and orientation. They vanish; we cannot rely on them to know what is going on. We experience something that cannot be represented or known in usual ego ways; it is unknowable through familiar routes of words or images. We feel in it, not knowing about it. We feel dumb and aware we are in something bigger that we cannot adequately observe and define.

For Nicholas our greatest learning is to dismantle any smug sense we can know and approach God from our side, so to speak, through reason, imagination, sight, knowledge, human methods. For God is incomprehensible. We must learn to see and accept "our learned ignorance" "that in which knowing is knowing that one is not able to know"; this "furnishes revelatory insight into the reality of things that properly lie beyond human comprehension" (ibid, 338, 339). In Jungian terms, we might suggest, the ego sees its ways of knowing cannot extend to the Self mode of knowing. Coming to this awareness is like clearing brush away to see there is another mode of knowing that comes from itself, not from the ego.

2. Secondly, for Jung, our firsthand knowledge of coincidence of noncausally related opposites is central to experiences of synchronicity that give evidence of a psychoid nature of meaning as existing *a priori* to human consciousness with its categories of space, time, causality. This meaningfulness exists objectively outside us in matter. We become aware through our psychological subjective registering of its impact and import that such meaningfulness exists. For Nicholas coincidence of opposites shows what is beyond coincidence, shows how God appears in the world and the method we can use to know God. Coincidence of contradictories is the door through the wall of paradise on the other side of which God exists objectively, but we know that only through our subjective experience of going through that door and registering that God exists beyond it. Coincidence of opposites is the method of perceiving God who shows Godself in such coincidences and the meaning it reveals.

3. Thirdly, for Jung experiences of synchronicity in which coincidence of opposites is central, open us to or open to us what Jung calls the *unus mundus,* the one world, a larger unity that holds everything (Jung 1958/1964a, para 778). This relates to the theme of *Anima Mundi*, soul of the world, in which interconnection of all things is held within an embracing wholeness, that I emphasize as matrix that penetrates all things and shows all things to interpenetrate. (We might speculate that this interpenetrating matrix feels different from a 'container' in which objects are put. An

interpenetrating matrix registers in us as all objects (and subjects) are already in a wholeness that communicates back and forth in its diverse 'parts'.) Jung says, the "*unus mundus* is a metaphysical speculation", a postulate of "a unitary aspect of being" (Jung 1963, paras 660, 663). Experience of this larger entirety and of the meaningfulness that all of life is interdependent can bridge the division on an individual level between what Jung calls personality 1 and personality 2, and on a collective level the graver, wider "gulf that seems unfathomable: the apparently irremediable separation of spirit from nature and the body" (ibid, para 664). Thus in this 'speculation' Jung, drawing on alchemy, on psychoid quality of the unconscious, and on notion of synchronicity, moves to correct the sundering of *materia* and *pneuma*. Indeed, this 'speculation' moves toward healing the rift between mind and body, psyche and soma, and in its larger ramifications between human and divine, creation and creator.

A smaller but decisive example of the consequences of such a split is especially evident in the skewing of symbols of masculine and feminine into hierarchical placement of feminine as of inferior substance and secondary creation (created after Adam and from his body), leaving the feminine identified with evil and matter. Twentieth century movements of feminism and earth consciousness (Gaia, green) and twenty-first century emphasis on awareness of gender fluidity, and no-gender identification are examples of efforts to overcome this gulf that shows itself in grievous prejudice, persecution (Baring and Cashford 1991, 423,434, 439, 441, 508, 518, 522, 524, 532-536, 543; see also page 62 above).

The felt meaningfulness of this ultimate unity that we cannot know but can glimpse, has implications for daily life, for clinical practice, and for change in our basic way of seeing reality. On levels of daily life and clinical practice we reckon with presence of unconscious depth that can be experienced but not known, not represented or imaged until it approaches consciousness: "we have no certain knowledge. The concept of psychic wholeness necessarily implies an element of transcendence on account of the existence of unconscious components. Transcendence in this sense is not equivalent to a metaphysical postulate ... it claims to be no more than a borderline concept." But, "there is something beyond the borderline, beyond the frontiers of knowledge ... shown by the archetypes" (Jung, 1958/1964a, para 780). Jung cites numbers as examples of this frontier quality that "on this side of the border are quantities but on the other side are autonomous psychic entities, capable of making qualitative statements which manifest themselves in *a priori* patterns of order." In the unitary world, it makes sense "that the living matter has a psychic aspect, and the psyche a physical aspect ... to suppose that every physical event would involve a psychic one and vice versa" (ibid).

The impact of perception of this wholeness is tremendous. We feel its presence in an undifferentiated way in experience of the psychoid quality of the unconscious; it brings a grounding experience of the what, the something more over the border. Consciousness of this assemblage (the unitary world) is the goal, a leap perhaps to new perception of reality (see page 69 above). In the glimpse of this ensemble in experiences of synchronicity we connect with our place in it; we find where we belong.

Monick makes a useful distinction: "The unitary world and its transgressive quality are functional in the *unus mundus* as in the psychoid unconscious, but with a significant difference. In the psychoid unconscious, unitary and transgressive qualites of the psyche exist in a condition of primitive nondifferentation. *Unus Mundus*, however, is a state of awareness where division and cohesion in the cognitive process are no longer understood only as streams of energy moving in opposite directions ... but are complementary, moving along the same path.... It strives to bring together differentiated opposites in a prospective unitary direction ... into synthesis, the point beyond the struggle for differentiation" (Monick 1987, 64, 66).

For Nicholas through and beyond the wall of coincidence of opposites that removes our obstructing knowledge, we see God who is all in all, the possibility, the 'Can-That-Is' in each and every thing, without which nothing can exist. All reality – us, and every existent thing – resides in God as infinity. All contradictories are in God, unity of diversity. Seeing unity is seeing God who is beyond all opposites. For Jung, through experience of the psychoid, the coincidence of opposites, the unity glimpsed through synchronicity, comes our sense of self-subsistent meaning exterior to us that we do not produce though we participate in its becoming real to us in our symbolization of it.

4) Fourthly, for Jung, the meaning of seeing the *unus mundus* deeply impresses us, connects us to the entirety beyond space, time, causality. These are experiences we may never understand, but never forget. They impress themselves upon us. They are life-changing, often noted with 'before' and 'after' temporality, and an 'I knew, I saw' cognition. Such events give a sense of the 'what' to which we belong. There is meaningfulness that exists in itself, objectively outside us, and we feel its impact deep inside us. We also sense we participate in creating this meaning in working to symbolize what happens to us in the psychoid level of experience and in synchronicity experiences.

Consciousness of this wholeness of interdependence is a mark of individuation, I suggest. I understand it to mean not so much that we become whole as it is we find our connection to and dependence on this completeness, this unitary reality. Individuation is an ongoing process, never done. Those in it influence others, almost as if multiplying the openness to grow, to include all that belongs to oneself, to feel full force of human emotions of which we are capable. Such a process is affective; it exerts its effects upon us, on how we think, orient to the meaning of life, relate to it in ourselves and with others. It is as if such experience presses on us to know it.

For Nicholas he finds the God-image that bestows happiness on him and shows God as Possest, *quiddity*, the "Can-That-Is", that is in everything, without which nothing can be. He sees into the mystery at the center of reality and knows he is related to it, and it is related to him. Because God is in every thing, creature, and person, Nicholas sees God turning toward us, coming after us, wanting us to know God in every sense, even touch and texture, taste and fragrance as well as reason and imagination. But God is not any of these; these are in God: "in God all things are God, there the joy of all pleasures that we derive from the eyes, ears, taste, touch, smell, life, motion, reason, and intelligence is the infinite, divine, and inexpressible joy and final rest of all pleasure and delight, for God is *Theos,* Vision, and Discursus, who sees all things, is in all things, and runs through all things ... the beginning from which everything flows forth, the middle in which we move, and the end to which everything flows back again, is everything" (ibid, 222-223). A joyousness imbues Nicholas' sentences, a plenty, a gladness in discovering the true source of our living. He sees sin as obstruction, and does not dwell on the crucifixion, but on the incarnation in Christ: "The God-human is the supreme coincidence."[11] (ibid, 25; see also 272-278, 281-282). Nicholas looks to the great reconciliation of the gap between human and divine, nature and spirit, the created order and its author (ibid, 55).

5) Fifthly, for Jung, we can discern ways of the Self in contrast to and in conjunction with ways of the ego. Those pivotal experiences of the psychoid and of synchronicity initiate such ventures that can unfold into life-long path – the what to which we devote heart soul and mind and strength. But such a path demands looking into, not to lasso the Self to ego projects. For then we experience Self as defeat of ego (Jung 1963, para 778). We can register Self precincts if we want, but not as ego knowledge. Our great conflicts center around the friction and fracture of ego and Self modes. The two ways always require delicate, persistent, inquiring, curious, sustained, devoted attentiveness to see how the alignment of the two might come about, grow flexible into the health of 'elbow-room,' to live our life's melody including the spaces in between the notes.

11. Nicholas is passionate about Jesus and the Christ as "the most perfect appearance of *Posse* Itself" (Nicholas of Cusa 1997, 68). As H. Lawrence Bond, his translator and interpreter says of Nicholas' understanding of Christ, "The hypostatic union of the two natures of his person is the perfect coincident, without mixture, composition, or proportion between the two parts – a coincident union without transference of either component. Coincidence on this model embraces distinction and unity."(ibid, 54-55; see also 276ff, 288-89).

For Nicholas, God wants us to know Godself (Nicholas 1997, 226). God gives knowledge to those who seek not just knowledge of God but to those "who 'seek life,' which is God, who seek not just the experience of God, but God Godself"' (ibid, 42, 228). That difference describes the further step a lover of God takes. We seek God for the sake of Godself, not for knowledge of God, nor to have the experience of God. We thus become the symbol that points to, honors, contemplates, shows the glory (in Nicholas' terms) of The-Can-Is, the *Possest* (ibid, 47). Like Jung, Nicholas sees the only way to point to God who surpasses our knowing is through symbols. As H.L. Bond sums it up: "With Cusa, theology cannot describe God's essence, and the theologian searching after symbol and imagery is oneself symbol and image. The theologian is living symbol" (ibid, 52).

Despite differences of terms, of centuries, and of traditions, we can see why Jung uses Nicholas to bolster his own revelations. Jung creatively adapts others' thought to pursue his own creative vision. He is not giving an outline of the thought of e.g. Kant or Nicholas of Cusa or even of the Golden Flower essay he found so crucial to the development of his thought (Jung 1957/1967 paras 1,18, 3; Jung 1957/1967b, para 96; Jaffé 1963, 197). He adapts what flashes to him in another's ideas and tradition to amplify the glimpses of the beyond he spies.

The danger, I suggest, is when we, after Jung, rely on him for what Kant said, or what the Golden Flower text means in the history of Taoism, or to exegete Nicholas of Cusa's theology. We must work up our own study of those documents and thinkers in their own contexts. Jung is not in the business of teaching another scholar's body of work. He is after the tiger his own vision espies and he appropriates its stripes wherever he catches sight of them.[12]

12. For example, Jung recognizes Nicholas' God-image in a neighborly nearness to the image of the Mercurial Fountain Jung investigates in *The Psychology of the Transference*: "the circular sea with no outlet, which perpetually replenishes itself by means of a spring bubbling up in its centre, is to be found in Nicholas of Cusa as an allegory of God" (Jung 1946/1954, para 409). Noting that Nicholas is "a contemporary of our alchemists" Jung connects his emphasis on "water as a symbol of wisdom and spirit" with

Suggested Implications of Aspects of Nicholas' Notion of Godself in Us for Jung's Notion of Self

To attend to connections between ideas of Nicolas of Cusa and Jung suggests to me two major implications. The first is given by Nicholas' notion of Godself living in us and how it may amplify Jung's notion of Self and how it lives and operates in us.

Nicholas of Cusa says we cannot ever know God by ourselves. But God's light "illumines our ignorance," that is, we stay ignorant, having learned that knowing God surpasses our comprehension. But God is the "Can-Is' in each of us, including Godself within us, and God knows all things. Therefore we can know God through God in us knowing God. We know God through Godself in us knowing God, and we know God through God in us knowing Godself within us: "In God's light is all our knowledge, so that it is not we ourselves who know, but rather it is God who knows in us" (Nicholas of Cusa 1997, 41, 225).

Jung sees the Self living in us and interpenetrating with the ego, not containing; we need both ego and Self and in reciprocal relationship. Jung says images for God and the Self are indistinguishable, though, as is frequent in Jung, he does the opposite too, distinguishing them from time to time. Jung says, "The God-image is the expression of an underlying *experience of something* which I cannot attain to by intellectual means.... I know I have such experience also, which I call God.... 'I know Him.' But why should you call this something 'God' ? I would ask: 'Why not?' It has always been called "God." An excellent and very suitable name indeed" (Jung 1976, November 16 1959, to Valentine Brooks, 522-523).

I have understood the Self not as God within us, but that within us that knows about God (or what we put in place of God even if we say there is no such reality). I understand the Self to mediate between the psyche and beyond psyche, beyond consciousness

---

Nicholas' sermon on Christ speaking to the Samaritan woman at the well where Nicholas says (in Jung's translation from the Latin) "The living well ...calls the thirsty ...that they may be quickened with the water of healing wisdom" (ibid, para 485).

and beyond unconscious, both personal and collective, that we experience in psychoid quality of the unconscious as plenty, abundance, peace the saints know, or as that abyss and void that trauma inflicts. The Self mediates that which is beyond human psyche, all levels of it.

Another way Nicholas describes this knowing that goes on in us through Godself in us, is God as infinity – the infinity knowing itself through and in our finiteness. Nicholas perceives God wishing to be found and known by us (Nicholas 1997, 51). Jung's notion of Self also presses to be known and responds to the ego knowing it, so to speak (which is a difference between Jung's Self and Bion's O which, as I understand it, remains impersonal) (Jung 1959, para 303). Even further, Nicholas has the idea, indeed the experience, that in searching for God we are searched and sought. In discovering God behind our symbols we discover ourselves as symbols pointing to God. The infinite acting on us, penetrating us in our finitude is an instance of coincidence of opposites as a means of crossing the finite-infinite gap and a method to think about crossing the gap between infinite and finite, divine and human, of seeking and being sought.

Suggested Implications of Nicholas' God-Image for Jung's Complex

The first implication of Nicholas' notion of Godself in us and Jung's notion of Self in us is a neighborliness between these ideas. Both emphasize the function of symbols to reach toward what surpasses symbols. The proof of the there there – which both call God – is not in conceptual knowledge but in our living the discovery we in our symbolizing are symbols ourselves, pointing to what exceeds our comprehension but penetrates and is penetrated by this other, God or Self, through relationship with it.

There are differences, however, between Nicholas' God-image and Jung's notion of Self. A second area of implication concerns the complex with which I understand Jung to have struggled that shows itself in *The Red Book* in two important relationships: to do with the Self and God and to do with feminine, Eros, loving a woman, Salome. Central to both conflicts is what Jung calls his freedom to be and maintain his own subjectness and not be forced to comply with nor to restrict his freedom in allegiance to some coercive authority.

This complex shows itself poignantly in *The Red Book* in the mangled state of his soul portrayed in sightless, maddened, murderous Salome at the beginning of the volume who slowly transforms to a grounded loving woman who wants to give her love to Jung. He says, No! That would be an iron ring; it would stifle my freedom (Jung 2009, 324-325). He cannot reconcile his cherished freedom with loving intimacy with another. Jung finally resolves this impasse by devotion to love itself, not to a personal other (Jung 2009, 356). That is a great development from his original conflict with Salome in the book, but living freely as his ownmost self in loving intimacy with a real other eludes him.

The same kind of conflict arises in Jung in relation to gaining his self. (I understand self here in the text (ibid, 338) to mean his personal self mixed with his later concept of self as the center of the entire personality, conscious and unconscious.) Can he have a self if he has a relation with God whose all in allness could swallow up his subjectness and snuff his freedom to be a subject. Remember Jung's dream with his father conducting Jung to "the highest presence", but first his father bows his head all the way to the ground. Jung does the same, but reserves a millimeter between his head and the ground to protect his freedom (Jaffé 1963, 219). Need for that invaluable human freedom remains with Jung in relation to God. The ego has its own precious place and to give it over entirely to a greater authority is to lose its independent capacity.

In *The Red Book* Jung describes this delicate and complicated relationship of self to God and the necessity to secure a place for the self in its own stance. "The God appears to us in a certain state of the soul. Therefore we reach God through the self. Not the self is God.... The God is behind the self, above the self.... But he appears as our sickness, from which we must heal ourselves." Jung's pivotal point comes in the following: "For in the first instance the God's power resides entirely in the self, since the self is completely in the God, because we were not with the self. Therefore we must wrestle with the God for the self. Since God is an unfathomable powerful movement that sweeps away the self into the boundless, into dissolution" (Jung 2009, 338). Philemon then tells Jung, "The God should not live in you, but you should live in the God" (ibid, 239). I understand this to mean we must first have a self in ego terms and in terms of ego relating to self before we can choose to offer our self to God, or choose not to do so. If the God lives in us we are drowned in the all in all; hence we must bring the self over to our human side, our small but valuable human freedom to be a subject with agency, however tiny.

In contrast, Nicholas of Cusa discovers that his freedom to be himself lies in God, that they interpenetrate; it is not possible to have one without the other. To choose and treasure one's own freedom, to find one's real self, true self, ownmost self, is possible, indeed made possible by Godself: "O Lord ... you have placed within my freedom that I be my own if I am willing. Hence, unless I am my own, you are not mine, for ... you cannot be mine unless I am also mine" (ibid, 247). The opposites of God and self that Jung struggles with, Nicholas sees as coinciding in Godself. Godself lives in us and is the means we even know there is a Godself. To choose self is to choose Godself and the opposite is true as well; they are interdependent; they interpenetrate. *Posse*, God, wants us, indeed, follows us, to turn toward God in order to live happily, to live this interpenetration (ibid, 242). Nicholas knows he is free to love God or not (ibid, 271), and that unless "I am my own you are not mine", and that God says to him "you be yours and I too will be yours" (ibid, 18-19, 247).

God shows a way to full resolution of any conflict about losing ourself if we love God all out, or losing God if we choose to sustain our own subjectivity. Nicholas gets it, speaks it: "O God ... no one can approach you because you are unapproachable ... you who are all in all ... how will you give me yourself if you do not also give me myself? ... you, Lord answer me within my heart, saying: "Be yours and I will too be yours ... unless I am my own, you are not mine ... you wait for me to choose to be my own" (ibid). No wonder Nicholas feels happiness!

References

Addison, A. 2009. "Jung, vitalism and 'the psychoid'; an historical reconstruction" in *Journal of Analytical Psychology* 54, 1, 123-143.

— 2011. "Jung's psychoid concept and Bion's protomental concept: a comparison" in Journal of Analytical Psychology 61, 5, 567-588.

Atwood, G. E. 2014. *The Abyss of Madness.* New York: Routledge.

Balint, E. 1993. *Before I was I: Psychoanalysis and Imagination.* Eds. Juliet Mitchell, Michael Parsons. London: Free Association Books and New York: The Guilford Press.

Baring, A. and Cashford, J. 1991. *The Myth of the Goddess, Evolution of an Image.* London: Arkana, Penguin Books.

Bedi, A. 2013. "India: an odyssey of individuation of an ancient civilization" in *Jung and India.* New Orleans, La.: *Spring A Journal of Archetype and Culture,* 105-125.

Bion, W.R. 1967/1984. *Second Thoughts.* London: Karnac.

— 1991. *A Memoir of the Future.* London: Karnac.

— 1992. *Cogitations.* London: Karnac.

Bright, G. 2014. "Jung's concept of psychoid unconsciousness: a clinician's view" in *Transformation, Jung's Legacy and Clinical Work Today.* Eds. Alessandra Cavalli, Lucinda Hawkins, and Martha Stevns. London: Karnac, 81-107.

Brooks, R. Mc. 2011. "Un-thought out metaphysics in analytical psychology: a critique of Jung's epistemological basis for psychic reality" in *Journal of Analytical Psychology* 56, 4, 492-514.

Caputo, J. D. 2011. "Hospitality and the trouble with God" in *Phenomenology and the Stranger Between Hostility and Hospitality.* Eds. Richard Kearney and Kascha Semenovitch. New York: Fordham University Press, 83-97.

Carvalho, R. 2014. "A vindication of Jung's unconscious and its archetypal expression: Jung, Bion, and Matte Blanco" in *Transformation, Jung's Legacy and Clinical Work Today.* Eds. Alessandra Cavalli, Lucinda Hawkins and Martha Stevns, 31-59.

Cavalli, A. 2014. "From not-knowing to knowing: on early infantile trauma involving separation" in *Transformation, Jung's Legacy and Clinical Work Today.* Eds. Alessandra Cavalli, Lucinda Hawkins and Martha Stevns. London: Karnac, 193-213.

Collins, A. and Molchanov, E. 2013. "Churning the Milky Ocean: poison and nectar in Carl Jung's India" in *Jung in India. Spring A Journal of Archetype and Culture* 90, Fall, 23-77.

Colman, W. 2011. "Synchroncity and the meaning-making psyche" in *Journal of Analytical Psychology 56*, 4, 471-492.

Cross, F. I. and Livingstone, E. A. 1974. Eds. *Oxford Dictionary of the Christian Church.* New York: Oxford University Press.

Davoine, F. and Gaudilliere, J-M. 2004. *History Beyond Trauma.* Trans. Susan Fairfield. New York: Other Books Press.

Dickinson, E. 1890/1960. "Bloom-is-result to meet a flower" in *The Complete Poems of Emily Dickinson.* Ed. Thomas A. Johnson. Boston: Little, Brown, and Company, poem 1058.

Dyer, D. R. 2000. *Jung's Thoughts on God Religious Depths of the Psyche.* York Beach Maine: Nicolas-Hayes.

Edinger, E. F. *Goethe's Faust Notes for a Jungian Commentary.* Toronto: Inner City Books.

— 1995. *The Mysterium Lectures A Journey Through C. G. Jung's Mysterium Coniunctionis.* Trans. and ed. Joan Dexter Blackner. Toronto: Inner City Books.

Emmet, D. M. 1957. *The Nature of Metaphysical Thinking.* New York: MacMillan.

Felstiner, J. 2001. *Paul Celan Poet, Survivor, Jew.* New Haven: Yale University Press.

Flamm, J. D. 1978. *Matisse on Art.* New York: E.P. Dutton.

Fordham, M. 1995. "Critical Note of Meltzer's *The Kleinian Development*" in *Freud, Jung, Klein – The Fenceless Field: Essays on Psychoanalysis and Analytical Psychology*. Ed. R. Hobdell. London: Routledge.

— 1974. "Defences of the self" in *Journal of Analytical Psychology* 19, 2, 192-199.

Gerson, S. 2009. "When the third is dead. Memory, mourning, and witnessing in the aftermath of the Holocaust" in *International Journal of Psychoanalysis* 2009, 90, 1341-1357, in Book Review by Ken Kimmel, *Journal of Analytical Psychology* September 2011, 56, 5, 571-574.

Godsil, G. 2014. "Reversal and recovery in trauma: unrepresentability in Bion, Jung, and Fordham" in *Transformations, Jung's Legacy and Clinical Work Today*. Eds. Alessandra Cavalli, Lucinda Hawkins and Martha Stevns. London: Karnac, 59-79.

Green, A. 1993. *On Private Madness*. Madison, Ct.: International Universities Press.

Green, A. 2000. *André Green at the Squiggle Foundation*. Ed. Jan Abram. London: Karnac.

Hennecke, E. 1964. *The New Testament Apocrypha*. Ed. Wilhelm Schneemelcher. Ed. and English Translation R. McL. Wilson. Philadephia: Westminster Press.

Hollywood, A. 1995. *The Soul as Virgin Wife*. Notre Dame: University of Notre Dame Press.

Jaffé, A. 1963. *Memories, Dreams, Reflections by C.G. Jung*. Trans. Richard and Clara Winston. New York: Pantheon.

— 1971/1989. *From the Life and Work of C.G. Jung*. Einsiedeln, Switzerland: Daimon Verlag.

Jung, C. G. 1921/1971. *Psychological Types. Collected Works* 6. Trans. R. F. C. Hull. Princeton, N. J.: Princeton University Press.

— 1926/1960. "Spirit and Life" in *The Structure and Dynamics of the Psyche. Collected Works* 8. Trans. R. F. C. Hull. New York: Pantheon, paras 601-648.

— 1928/1954. "The Therapeutic Reaction of Abreaction" in *The Practice of Psychotherapy. Collected Works* 16. Trans. R. F. C. Hull. New York: Pantheon, paras 255-293.

— 1931/1954. "Marriage as a Psychological Relationship" in *The Development of the Personality. Collected Works* 17. New York: Pantheon, paras 189-345.

— 1933/1958. "Psychotherapists or the Clergy" in *Psychology and Religion: West and East. Collected Works* 11. Trans. R. F. C. Hull. New York: Pantheon, paras 488-538.

— 1934/1960. "The Soul and Death" in *CW* 8. New York: Pantheon, paras 796-815.

— 1946/1954. "Psychology of the Transference" in *CW* 16. Trans. R. F. C. Hull. New York: Pantheon, paras 163-321.

— 1948/1959. "The Phenomenology of the Spirit in Fairytales" in *The Archetypes of the Collective Unconscious. Collected Works* 9i. Trans. R. F. C. Hull. New York: Pantheon, paras 384-254.

— 1950a/1959. "Concerning Rebirth" *CW* 9i, paras 199-258.

— 1950b/1959. "Concerning Mandala Symbolism" in *CW* 9i, paras 627-712.

— 1950/1966. "Psychology and Literature" in *Collected Works* 15, *The Spirit* in *Man, Art, and Literature.* Trans. R. F. C. Hull. New York: Pantheon, paras 133-162.

— 1952/1960. "*Synchronicity: An Acausal Connecting Principle*" in *CW* 8, paras 816-997.

— 1953/1966. *Two Essays in Analytical Psychology. Collected Works* 7, Trans. R. F. C. Hull. New York: Pantheon.

— 1953. *Psychology and Alchemy. Collected Works* 12. Trans. R. F. C. Hull. New York: Pantheon.

— 1954/1958. "Transformation Symbolism in the Mass" in *CW* 11, paras 296-448.

— 1954/1960. "On the Nature of the Psyche" in *CW* 8, paras 343-442.

— 1954/1976. "Letter to Père Lachat" in *Collected Works* 18. Trans. R. F. C. Hull. Princeton, N.J.: Princeton University Press, paras 1532-1557.

— 1956-57/1976. "Jung and Religious Belief" in *CW* 18, paras 1584-1690.

— 1956/1974. *Symbols of Transformation. Collected Works 5.* Trans. R. F. C. Hull. Princeton, N.J.: Princeton University Press.

— 1957/1964. "The Undiscovered Self" in *Collected Works* 10 *Civilization in Transition*. Trans. R. F. C. Hull. New York: Pantheon, paras 488-588.

— 1957/1966. "Richard Wilhelm: in memoriam" in *CW* 15, paras 74-96.

— 1957/1967. "Commentary on 'The Secret of the Golden Flower'" in *Alchemical Studies. Collected Works* 13. Trans. R. F. C. Hull. Princeton, N. J.: Princeton University Press, paras 1-84.

— 1958a/1964. "Flying saucers: a modern myth of things in the skies" in *CW* 10, paras 589-824.

— 1958b/1964. "A psychological view of conscience" in *CW* 10, paras 825-857.

— 1959. *Aion Researches into the Phenomenology of the Self. Collected Works* 9ii. Trans. R. F. C. Hull. New York : Pantheon.

— 1963. *Mysterium Coniunctionis. Collected Works* 14. Trans. R. F. C. Hull. New York: Pantheon.

— 1976. *C. G. Jung Letters 1951-1961* v. 2 of 2. Eds. Gerhard Adler, Aniela Jaffé. Trans. R. F. C. Hull. Princeton, N. J.: Princeton University Press.

— 1984. *Dream Analysis, Notes of the Seminar Given in 1928-1930.* Ed. William McGuire. Princeton, N. J.: Princeton University Press.

— 2009. *The Red Book Liber Novus.* Ed. Sonu Shamdasani. Trans. Mark Kyburz, John Peck, and Sonu Shamdasani. New York: W.W. Norton.

Kohon, G. Ed. 1999. *The Dead Mother, The Work of Andre Green.* London: Routledge.

Kristeva J. 1988. "On melancholic imagination" in *Postmodernism and Continental Philosophy.* Eds. Hugh J. Silverman and Donn Welton. Albany, N. Y.: State University of New York, 12-26.

McAlister, M. 2014. "Beneath the skin: archetypal activity in psychosis" in *Transformation, Jung's Legacy and Clinical Work Today.* Eds. Alessandra Cavalli, Lucinda Hawkins, and Martha Stevns. London: Karnac, 155-177.

McIntosh, J. 2004. *Nimble Believing, Dickinson and the Unknown.* Ann Arbor, Michigan: University of Michigan Press.

Main, R. 2004. *The Rupture of Time Synchronicity and Jung's Critique of Modern Western Culture.* London and New York: Routledge.

— 2007. *Revelations of Chance Synchronicity as Spiritual Experience.* Albany: State University of New York Press.

Marguerite of Porete. 1993. *The Mirror of Simple Souls.* Trans. and Introduction Ellen Babinsky. New York and Mahwah, N. J.: Paulist Press.

Meredith-Owen, W. 2009. "Tradition and originality in the transference: a Coleridgean commentary" in *Journal of Analytical Psychology* 54, 3, 359-379.

— 2014. "On visiting the opening chapters of *Memories, Dreams, Reflections*" in *Transformation, Jung's legacy and Clinical Work Today*. Eds. Alessandra Cavalli, Lucinda Hawkins, and Martha Stevns. London: Karnac, 3-31.

Monick, E. 1987. *Phallos, Sacred Image of the Masculine*. Toronto: Inner City Books.

Murdoch, I. 1969. "On 'God' and the 'Good'" in *The Anatomy of Knowledge*. Ed. Marjorie Greene. Amherst, Mass.: The University of Massachusetts Press, 233-259.

Nicholas of Cusa. 1997. *Nicholas of Cusa, Selected Spiritual Writings*. Trans and Introduction H. Lawrence Bond. New York, Mahwah, N. J.: Paulist Press.

Randall, L. 2011. *Knocking on Heaven's Door, How Physics and Scientific Thinking Illuminate the Universe and the Modern World*. New York: Harper Collins.

— 2013. *The Higgs Bosin The Power of Empty Space*. New York: Harper Collins.

Saban, M. 2013. "Ambiguating Jung" in *How and Why We Still Read Jung*. Eds. Jean Kirsch and Murray Stein. New York: Routledge, 6-26.

Sedgwick, E. K. 2011. *The Weather in Proust*. Ed. Jonathan Goldberg. Durham and London: Duke University Press.

Spielrein, S. 1994. "Destruction in the cause of coming into being" in *Journal of Analytical Psychology* 39, 2, 155-187.

Stein, L. 2013. "Jung and Tantra" in *Jung and India. Spring Journal of Archetype and Culture* 90, Fall, 179-207.

Stein, M. 2014. *Minding the Self Jungian Meditations on Contemporary Spirituality*. London and New York: Routledge.

Sullivan, B. S. 2010. *The Mystery of Analytical Work, Weavings from Jung and Bion*. New York: Routledge.

Stokes, A. 1972. *The Image in the Form Selected Writings of Adrian Stokes*. Ed. Richard Wolheim. New York: Harper Collins.

Ulanov, A. and Ulanov, B. 1975. *Religion and the Unconscious*. Louisville Ky: John Knox Westminster Press.

— and — 1991/1999. *The Healing Imagination.* Einsiedeln, Switzerland: Daimon Verlag.

Ulanov, A. B. 1971. *The Feminine in Jungian Psychology and in Christian Theology.* Evanston, Il.: Northwestern University Press.

— 1984/2005: "The God you touch" in *Spirit in Jung.* Einsiedeln, Switzerland: Daimon Verlag, 259-287.

— 1992/2005. "Jung and prayer" in *Spirit in Jung*, 25-55.

— 1994. *The Wizards' Gate, Picturing Consciousness.* Einsiedeln, Switzerland: Daimon Verlag.

— 1996a. "Disguises of the anima" in *The Functioning Transcendent.* Wilmette, Il.: Chiron, 159-190.

— 1996b. "Spiritual aspects of clinical work" in *The Functioning Transcendent, 3-23.*

— 1996/2004. "Ritual, repetition, and psychic reality" in *Spiritual Aspects of Clinical Work.* Einsiedeln, Switzerland: Daimon Verlag, 392-424.

— 1998/2004. "The gift of consciousness" in *Spiritual Aspects of Clinical Work,* 197-221.

— 2000/2004. "Psychotherapy and spirituality" in *Spiritual Aspects of Clinical Work,* 74-108.

— 2001a. *Finding Space: Winnicott, God, and Psychic Reality.* Louisville, Ky: John Knox Westminster Press.

— 2001b. *Attacked by Poison Ivy A Psychological Understanding.* York Beach, Maine; Nicolas-Hayes.

— 2007. "The third in the shadow of the fourth" in *Journal of Analytical Psychology* 52, 5, 585-607.

— 2008/2014. "Is there a there there, or is this the wrong question?" in *Knots and Their Untying, Essays on Psychological Dilemmas.* New Orleans, La.: Spring Journal Books, 163-181.

— 2009/2014. "What do we do if we cannot forgive? If forgiveness does not happen?" in *Knots and Their Untying, Essays in Psychological Dilemmas,* 183-217.

— 2012/2015. "Jung, Psychic reality, and God" in *Jung in the Academy and Beyond.* Eds. Mark E. Mattson, Frederick J. Wertz, Harry Fogarty, Margaret Klenck, Beverley Zabriskie. New Orleans, La.: Spring Journal Books, 165-186.

— 2013. *Madness & Creativity.* College Station, TX: Texas A & M Press.

— 2013/2014. "Jerusalem" in *Knots and Their Untying, Essays in Psychological Dilemmas,* 217-233.

Winnicott, D. W. 1963/1989. "Fear of breakdown" in *Psycho-analytic Explorations.* Eds. Clare Winnicott, Ray Shepherd, Madeleine Davis. London: Karnac, 87-95.

— 1968/1989. "Development of the theme of the mother's mind as discussed in psycho-analytic practice" in *Psychoanalytic Explorations,* 247-260.

— 1970/1986. "Living creatively" in *Home is Where We Start From.* New York: W. W, Norton, 35-55.

— 1971. *Playing and Reality.* London: Tavistock.

— 1988. *Human Nature.* London: Free Association Books.

Wirtz, U. 2014. *Trauma and Beyond, The Mystery of Transformation.* New Orleans, La.: Spring Journal Books.

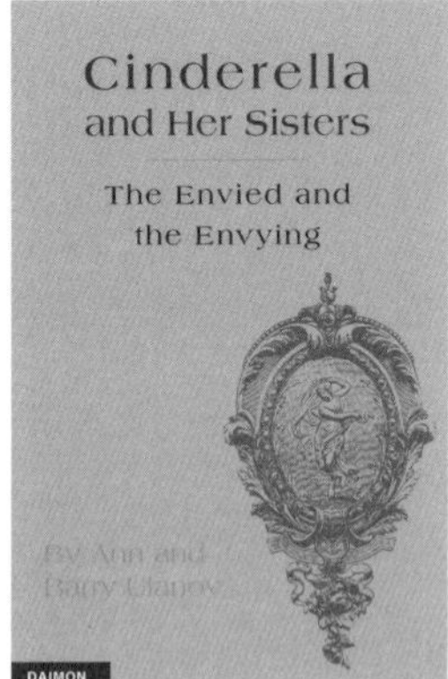

Ann & Barry Ulanov

Cinderella and Her Sisters

The Envied and the Envying

Seated in her nest of ashes, Cinderella embodies human misery. The essence of inner and outer nobility, she is the envy of her cruel stepmother and her ugly sisters. Using this familiar story, Ann and Barry Ulanov explore the psychological and theological aspects of envy and goodness. In their interpretation of the tale, they move back and forth between internal and external issues – from how feminine and masculine parts of persons fit or do not fit together to how individuals conduct their lives with those of the same and opposite sexes, how they conflict, compete, or join harmoniously.

"The Cinderella tale, so simple and so profound, offers a direct road into and through the thickets of envying and being envied. Envy between sisters, between mothers and daughters, between the sexes, between nations . . . between different parts of our own psyche, even of God – these are the multiple places of wounding we touch in this book. The central role of envy in determining the very nature of our society – its politics, for example – is, we think, crucial."

200 pages, 3rd edition, ISBN 978-3-85630-746-2

Ann Ulanov

Spiritual Aspects of Clinical Work

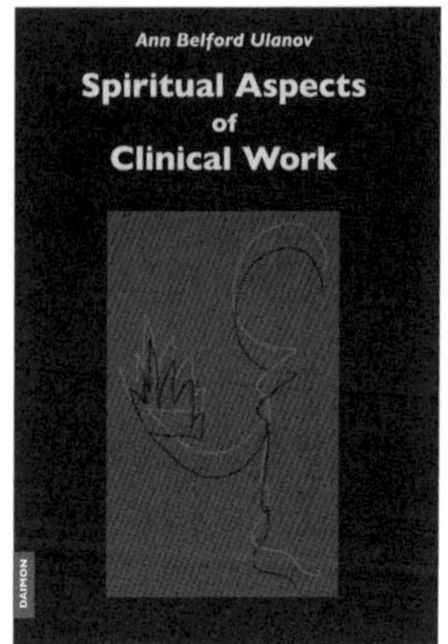

How does the spirit come into clinical work? Through the analyst? In the analysand's work in the analysis? What happens to human destructiveness if we embrace a vision of non-violence? Do dreams open us to spiritual life? What is the difference between repetition compulsion and ritual? How does religion feed terrorism? What happens if analysts must wrestle with hate in themselves? Do psychotherapy and spirituality compete, or contradict, or converse with each other? What does religion uniquely offer, beyond what psychoanalysis can do, to our surviving and thriving?

480 pages, ISBN 978-3-85630-634-2

Haruki Murakami goes to meet Hayao Kawai

Two of Japan's foremost contemporary cultural spokespersons met for an informal conversation with remarkable results. While their extended talk took place at a particular location at a particular moment in history, much of the content is timeless and universal. After popular acclaim in Japan, the transcript now makes its first appearance in English.

Topics from the Contents:

The Meaning of Commitment
Words or Images?
Making Stories
Answering Logically versus Answering Compassionately
Self-Healing and Novels
Marriage and 'Well-digging'
Curing and Living
Stories and the Body
The Relationship between a Work and its Author
Individuality and Universality
Violence and Expression
Where are We Headed?

160 pages, hardcover, ISBN 978-3-85630-764-6

E.A. Bennet

Meetings with Jung

In this collection of diary entries made by British psychiatrist E.A. Bennet during his visits with the Swiss analyst C.G. Jung over a 15-year period, Bennet's colorfully spontaneous accounts reveal Jung's down-to-earth personality and his extraordinary mind, at ease in his daily surroundings. Meetings with Jung serves as an ideal introduction to Jungian psychology while providing a rare, intimate perspective into Jung's life and work for those already familiar with the more scholarly literature.

125 pages, ISBN 978-3-85630-501-7

English Titles from Daimon

Ruth Ammann - *The Enchantment of Gardens*
Susan R. Bach - *Life Paints its Own Span*
Diana Baynes Jansen - *Jung's Apprentice: A Biography of Helton Godwin Baynes*
John Beebe (Ed.) - *Terror, Violence and the Impulse to Destroy*
E.A. Bennet - *Meetings with Jung*
W.H. Bleek / L.C. Lloyd (Ed.) - *Specimens of Bushman Folklore*
Tess Castleman - *Threads, Knots, Tapestries*
- *Sacred Dream Circles*
George Czuczka - *Imprints of the Future*
Renate Daniel - *Taking the Fear out of the Night*
Eranos Yearbook 69 - *Eranos Reborn*
Eranos Yearbook 70 - *Love on a Fragile Thread*
Eranos Yearbook 71 - *Beyond Masters*
Eranos Yearbook 72 - *Soul between Enchantment and Disenchantment*
Michael Escamilla - *Bleuler, Jung, and the Schizophrenias*
Heinrich Karl Fierz - *Jungian Psychiatry*
John Fraim - *Battle of Symbols*
von Franz / Frey-Rohn / Jaffé - *What is Death?*
Liliane Frey-Rohn - *Friedrich Nietzsche, A Psychological Approach*
Marion Gallbach - *Learning from Dreams*
Ralph Goldstein (Ed.) - *Images, Meanings & Connections: Essays in Memory of Susan Bach*
Yael Haft - *Hands: Archetypal Chirology*
Fred Gustafson - *The Black Madonna of Einsiedeln*
Daniel Hell - *Soul-Hunger: The Feeling Human Being and the Life-Sciences*
Siegmund Hurwitz - *Lilith, the first Eve*
Aniela Jaffé - *The Myth of Meaning*
- *Was C.G. Jung a Mystic?*
- *From the Life and Work of C.G. Jung*
- *Death Dreams and Ghosts*
C.G. Jung - *The Solar Myths and Opicinus de Canistris*
Verena Kast - *A Time to Mourn*
- *Sisyphus*
Hayao Kawai - *Dreams, Myths and Fairy Tales in Japan*
James Kirsch - *The Reluctant Prophet*
Eva Langley-Dános - *Prison on Wheels: Ravensbrück to Burgau*
Rivkah Schärf Kluger - *The Gilgamesh Epic*
Yehezkel Kluger & Naomi Kluger-Nash - *RUTH in the Light of Mythology, Legend and Kabbalah*
Paul Kugler (Ed.) - *Jungian Perspectives on Clinical Supervision*
Paul Kugler - *The Alchemy of Discourse*
Rafael López-Pedraza - *Cultural Anxiety*
- *Hermes and his Children*
Alan McGlashan - *The Savage and Beautiful Country*
Gregory McNamee (Ed.) - *The Girl Who Made Stars: Bushman Folklore*
- *The North Wind and the Sun & Other Fables of Aesop*
Gitta Mallasz - *Talking with Angels*
C.A. Meier - *Healing Dream and Ritual*
- *A Testament to the Wilderness*
- *Personality: The Individuation Process*
Haruki Murakami - *Haruki Murakami Goes to Meet Hayao Kawai*

English Titles from Daimon

Eva Pattis Zoja (Ed.)	- *Sandplay Therapy*
Laurens van der Post	- *The Rock Rabbit and the Rainbow*
Jane Reid	- *Jung, My Mother and I: The Analytic Diaries of Catharine Rush Cabot*
R.M. Rilke	- *Duino Elegies*
Miguel Serrano	- *C.G. Jung and Hermann Hesse*
Helene Shulman	- *Living at the Edge of Chaos*
D. Slattery / G. Slater (Eds.)	- *Varieties of Mythic Experience*
David Tacey	- *Edge of the Sacred: Jung, Psyche, Earth*
Susan Tiberghien	- *Looking for Gold*
Ann Ulanov	- *Spiritual Aspects of Clinical Work*
	- *Picturing God*
	- *The Female Ancestors of Christ*
	- *The Wisdom of the Psyche*
	- *The Wizards' Gate, Picturing Consciousness*
	- *The Psychoid, Soul and Psyche*
Ann & Barry Ulanov	- *Cinderella and her Sisters*
A. Schweizer / R. Scheizer-Villers	- *Stone by Stone: Reflections on Jung*
Eva Wertenschlag-Birkhäuser	- *Windows on Eternity: The Paintings of Peter Birkhäuser*
Harry Wilmer	- *How Dreams Help*
	- *Quest for Silence*
Luigi Zoja	- *Drugs, Addiction and Initiation*
Luigi Zoja & Donald Williams	- *Jungian Reflections on September 11*
Jungian Congress Papers	- *Jerusalem 1983: Symbolic & Clinical Approaches*
	- *Berlin 1986: Archetype of Shadow in a Split World*
	- *Paris 1989: Dynamics in Relationship*
	- *Chicago 1992: The Transcendent Function*
	- *Zürich 1995: Open Questions*
	- *Florence 1998: Destruction and Creation*
	- *Cambridge 2001*
	- *Barcelona 2004: Edges of Experience*
	- *Cape Town 2007: Journeys, Encounters*
	- *Montreal 2010: Facing Multiplicity*
	- *Copenhagen 2013: 100 Years on*

Our books are available from your bookstore or from our distributors:

AtlasBooks
30 Amberwood Parkway
Ashland OH 44805, USA
Phone: 419-281-5100
Fax: 419-281-0200
E-mail: order@atlasbooks.com
www.atlasbooks.com

Gazelle Book Services Ltd.
White Cross Mills, High Town
Lancaster LA1 4XS, UK
Tel: +44 1524 528500
Fax: +44 1524 528510
Email: sales@gazellebookservices.co.uk
www.gazellebookservices.co.uk

Daimon Verlag - Hauptstrasse 85 - CH-8840 Einsiedeln - Switzerland
Phone: (41)(55) 412 2266 Fax: (41)(55) 412 2231
Email: info@daimon.ch
Visit our website: **www.daimon.ch** *or write for our complete catalog*